Beyond
Peanut Butter
and Jelly

Time For Cooking

With the International Nanny Association

This cookbook is a collection of favorite recipes, which are not necessarily original recipes.

Beyond Peanut Butter and Jelly

Time for Cooking with the International Nanny Association

Published by the
International Nanny Association

Copyright 2000

International Nanny Association
900 Haddon Avenue, Suite 438
Collingswood, New Jersey 08108
www.nanny.org

Library of Congress Number: 99-072959
ISBN: 0-9673312-0-X

Edited, designed, and manufactured by
Favorite Recipes® Press
an imprint of

FRP

P.O. Box 305142
Nashville, Tennessee 37230

Book Design: Jim Scott
Art Director: Steve Newman
Project Manager: Ginger Ryan Dawson

Manufactured in the United States of America
First Printing: 2000   6,000 copies

Illustrator: Becky Kavanagh

This book is dedicated to children and families by those who support them—nannies, agencies, educators, and special services. No one understands the unique challenges of in-home child care better than we do. Together, we can make a difference for children.

You're the kind of nanny everyone will love, for you're a gift from Heaven high above.

You light up the sky, you bring down the moon, wherever you walk, flowers will bloom.

You make the day fun and you're never afraid, whenever we get cut, you know your first aid.

You passed every single nanny test.

Gee, in this job do you ever get a rest?

Love, Jenna Worsham, Age 11

Thank you for your love and care nannies, nannies everywhere.

There's something that I really want you to know—even when it rains, or even when it snows, or even when I'm mad at you,

I know inside that you really love me.

Thank you for me not being home alone because you are there when Mom is not at home.

When you are there I think inside, you are really MY nanny, with pride!

Marissa Peitzman, Age 6

The bread is spread, fingers stick,

a kiss on the head, handprints on the door;

Memories of packing lunch for the ones whom you adore.

The lessons learned, cap and gown, all full grown, and college bound;

Memories of a life packed full of love and more.

Beyond Peanut Butter and Jelly has good food, fun and games, and love of life sandwiched between its covers.

Our warmest thanks to those who contributed recipes, ideas, menus, and thoughts. This book represents only a portion of what we received. Due to space limitations and recipe similarities, all could not be printed in this book.

We gratefully acknowledge the authors of the sidebars sprinkled throughout this book. These favored and tested tidbits were compiled by friends, parents, and members of the International Nanny Association.

A special thanks to our illustrator, Becky Kavanagh, whose creative touches can be seen on these pages. Thanks for all your help and late night phone calls.

A special thanks to Sandra Costantino for her support, eye for detail, and desire for more information.

A special thanks to Kellie Geres whose long hours of help and patience did not go unnoticed. Glenda Durst and Connie White deserve a big thank you for easing the workload.

Special recognition goes to the Membership Services Office of the INA, specifically Diane O'Mara and Maryann Simila.

Karen Stuke, Resource Development Chair
International Nanny Association

CONTENTS

HISTORY

In 1985, nanny placement agency owners, nannies, and nanny educators from the United States, England, Canada, Australia, and New Zealand first gathered at Scripps College in Claremont, California. From this gathering, the International Nanny Association has evolved and experienced phenomenal growth over these past years as an association of individual members committed to professional in-home child care.

INA now serves as a clearinghouse for information on in-home child care. In the last 15 years, INA members have agreed on definitions for various in-home child care positions, recommended practices for nannies and nanny placement agencies, and prepared a comprehensive list of skills which educators can use in designing curriculum for nanny training programs.

6

TENDING THE GARDEN OF LIFE

Wake up early, full of energy.
For as the gardener, your day will be long.
Water with occasional tears of joy and sorrow.
Fertilize with love, as the soil will soak it up constantly.
Be patient, as the weeds of learning will creep.
Walk gently, for new growth sprouts underfoot.
May your smile radiate warmth and light.
Take time out, just to pause...
At the end of the day, reflect on the accomplishments.
For as the gardener, you nurture life!

INTRODUCTION

The International Nanny Association is a non-profit, educational association for nannies and those who educate, place, employ, and support professional in-home child care providers.

Membership is open to those who are directly involved with the in-home child care profession including nannies, nanny employers, nanny placement agency owners (and staff), nanny educators, and providers of special services related to the nanny profession.

Like you, we are concerned about quality child care. We have come together to help each other personally and professionally by sharing information and resources. Our unity as an association will prove invaluable in any regulation of our industry.

Since 1985, INA has worked steadily to promote professionalism among individuals involved with in-home child care. Our members voluntarily abide by the INA Commitment to Professional Excellence and the recommended practices that we have collectively developed for nannies, nanny placement agencies, and educators.

MUNCHIES AND MORE

APPETIZERS, SOUPS AND SALADS

Recipe for a Successful Nanny Career

1 cup of open communication

1 cup of flexibility

1 cup of patience

1 cup of love

Mix well and use generously

on a daily basis.

HARRIETTE GRANT—INA 1990 NANNY OF THE YEAR

BARBECUE MEATBALLS

3 1/4 pounds ground beef
2 eggs, lightly beaten
1 cup milk
1 cup rolled oats
1 cup chopped onion
1 teaspoon salt
3/4 teaspoon chili powder
1/2 teaspoon garlic powder
1/2 teaspoon pepper
4 cups catsup
1 cup packed brown sugar
1 cup chopped onion
2 tablespoons liquid smoke
1/2 teaspoon chili powder

Combine the ground beef, eggs, milk, oats, 1 cup onion, salt, 3/4 teaspoon chili powder, garlic powder and pepper in a bowl and mix well. Shape the ground beef mixture into 1-inch balls. Arrange in a 9x13-inch baking dish.

Combine the catsup, brown sugar, 1 cup onion, liquid smoke and 1/2 teaspoon chili powder in a bowl and mix well. Pour the catsup mixture over the prepared meatballs. Bake at 350 degrees for 1 hour.

Yield: 36 meatballs

Long plane ride in your future? Take along small, wrapped presents that children are allowed to open every hour on the plane. They can range from little toys to a book or small game. Children love to open packages!

Hot Pepper Jelly Appetizers

2 cups shredded Cheddar cheese
1 cup flour
6 tablespoons (3/4 stick) butter, chilled, chopped
1/2 cup hot pepper jelly

Combine the Cheddar cheese, flour and butter in a food processor container and process until the mixture resembles coarse meal. Process for an additional 5 to 6 seconds or until the mixture forms a ball.

Chill, wrapped in plastic wrap, for 30 minutes. Shape into 2-inch balls. Arrange 1 inch apart on an ungreased baking sheet.

Bake at 400 degrees for 5 minutes. Make a small indentation on the top of each ball. Spoon 1 teaspoon of the hot pepper jelly into each indentation. Bake for 5 minutes longer or until golden brown. Cool on the baking sheet for 2 minutes; remove to a wire rack to cool completely.

Yield: 24 servings

Cheese Coins

1 cup sifted flour
1/2 teaspoon salt
• Dash of cayenne
2 cups shredded sharp Cheddar cheese
1/2 cup (1 stick) butter or margarine, softened

Sift the flour, salt and cayenne into a bowl. Process the Cheddar cheese and butter in a food processor until creamy. Add the flour mixture and process until smooth. Divide the cheese mixture into 3 portions. Shape each portion into a log.

Chill, tightly wrapped in waxed paper, until firm. Cut into 1 1/3-inch slices. Arrange on a greased baking sheet. Bake at 400 degrees for 10 minutes or until light brown.

Yield: 6 servings

STUFFED JALAPEÑOS

1 pound ground sausage
2 cups finely shredded mild or medium Cheddar cheese
16 ounces cream cheese, softened
1 teaspoon steak seasoning
1 teaspoon Worcestershire sauce
1 (16-ounce) jar jalapeño chiles, halved, seeded

Brown the sausage in a skillet, stirring until crumbly; drain. Let stand until cool.

Combine the sausage, Cheddar cheese, cream cheese, steak seasoning and Worcestershire sauce in a bowl and mix well. Spoon the sausage mixture into the jalapeño chile halves, pressing firmly. Arrange on a serving platter.

Yield: 12 servings

SAUSAGE STARS

36 won ton wrappers
1 pound pork or turkey sausage
1 1/2 cups shredded sharp Cheddar cheese
1 1/2 cups shredded Monterey Jack cheese
1 cup ranch salad dressing
1 (2-ounce) can sliced black olives, drained
1/2 cup chopped red bell pepper

Spray 36 miniature muffin cups lightly with nonstick cooking spray. Press 1 won ton wrapper into each cup; spray with nonstick cooking spray. Bake at 350 degrees for 5 minutes or until golden brown. Remove from the muffin cups.

Arrange the won ton cups on a baking sheet. Brown the sausage in a skillet, stirring until crumbly; drain. Mix the sausage, Cheddar cheese, Monterey Jack cheese, salad dressing, olives and red pepper in a bowl. Spoon the sausage mixture into the won ton cups. Bake at 350 degrees for 5 minutes or until bubbly. May freeze the filled won ton cups for future use before baking.

Yield: 36 servings

SPINACH BALLS

2	(10-ounce) packages frozen chopped spinach, thawed, drained, patted dry
3	egg whites
2	eggs
2	cups Pepperidge Farm herb-seasoned stuffing mix
1	medium onion, finely chopped
3/4	cup light margarine
1/4	cup grated Parmesan cheese
1/2	tablespoon garlic powder
1/4	teaspoon pepper
1/4	teaspoon thyme or 1 teaspoon salt

Combine the spinach, egg whites, eggs, stuffing mix, onion, margarine, Parmesan cheese, garlic powder, pepper and thyme in a bowl and mix well. Shape the spinach mixture into 1-inch balls. Arrange on a baking sheet and freeze, covered.

Bake at 350 degrees for 25 to 30 minutes or until spinach balls are firm. May store in the freezer for future use before baking.

Yield: 50 servings

STUFFED MUSHROOMS

1/2	pound button mushrooms, stems removed
1/2	pound pork sausage
8	ounces cream cheese, softened
2	green onions, finely chopped
1/4	cup finely chopped walnuts
1	tablespoon sage
•	Paprika

Rinse the mushroom caps and pat dry. Brown the sausage in a skillet, stirring until crumbly; drain.

Combine the sausage, cream cheese, green onions, walnuts and sage in a bowl and mix well. Spoon the sausage mixture into the mushroom caps. Sprinkle with paprika. Arrange on a baking sheet.

Bake at 350 degrees until the cream cheese is melted and the mushroom caps are heated through.

Yield: 24 servings

Hot Crab Meat Dip

16   ounces cream cheese, softened
2   tablespoons chopped onion
1   tablespoon milk
1/2 tablespoon horseradish
1   teaspoon Worcestershire sauce
1/4 teaspoon salt
1/4 teaspoon pepper
•   Tabasco sauce to taste
1   pound fresh crab meat

Combine the cream cheese, onion, milk, horseradish, Worcestershire sauce, salt, pepper and Tabasco sauce in a mixer bowl and beat until blended. Stir in the crab meat.

Spoon the crab meat mixture into a baking dish. Bake at 375 degrees for 30 minutes. Serve warm.

Yield: 20 servings

Fresh Fruit Dip

8   ounces cream cheese, softened
1   (8-ounce) jar marshmallow creme
•   Grated fresh orange peel to taste
•   Powdered ginger to taste

Combine the cream cheese and marshmallow creme in a mixer bowl and beat until blended. Stir in the orange peel and ginger.

Chill, covered, in the refrigerator. Serve with fresh fruit such as apples, strawberries, kiwifruit and pineapple.

Yield: 2 cups

14

Mexican Layer Dip

1 (16-ounce) can refried beans
1 cup sour cream
• Chopped onion to taste
2 cups shredded Cheddar cheese
• Finely chopped lettuce to taste
1½ cups picante sauce
• Chopped tomato to taste
• Sliced green olives to taste

Spread the refried beans in a shallow 2½-quart dish. Layer the sour cream, onion, Cheddar cheese, lettuce, picante sauce, tomato and green olives in the order listed over the beans. Serve with tortilla chips.

May add taco-seasoned, browned ground beef between the sour cream and onion layers.

Yield: 12 servings

15

Stuffed animal collection out of control? A standard plastic planter holds a growing assortment of stuffed animals. Try the long and narrow ones that are used as window boxes. Mount it on a wall to keep the clutter off the floor.

Texas Trash Dip

1 (15-ounce) can field peas with snaps, drained
1 (15-ounce) can black-eyed peas with jalapeño chiles, drained
1 (8-ounce) bottle Italian salad dressing
1 (2-ounce) can sliced black olives, drained
2 tomatoes, chopped
1 avocado, chopped
1 small sweet onion, chopped
1 green bell pepper, chopped
• Chopped celery to taste

Combine the field peas, black-eyed peas, salad dressing, olives, tomatoes, avocado, onion, green pepper and celery in a bowl and mix well.

Chill, covered, for 8 to 10 hours. Serve with tortilla chips. May store in the refrigerator for 2 to 3 days.

Yield: 16 servings

Discontinued wallpaper books are great for all kinds of crafts. You can make bookmarks, cards, or book covers. Ask for them at various stores.

Rainbow Salsa

8	plum tomatoes or 3 tomatoes, seeded, diced
2	jalapeño chiles, seeded, diced
1	orange or yellow mild chile, diced
1/2	orange or yellow bell pepper, diced
6	to 8 scallions, chopped
•	Juice of 1 lime
1	teaspoon salt
•	Chopped cilantro (optional)

Combine the tomatoes, jalapeño chiles, mild chile and bell pepper in a bowl and mix well.

Stir in the scallions, half the lime juice and salt. Add the remaining lime juice, additional salt and cilantro to taste. Serve immediately with tortilla chips.

Yield: 10 servings

Roquefort Log

6	ounces cream cheese, softened
2	ounces Roquefort cheese, crumbled
2	tablespoons finely chopped celery
1	tablespoon minced onion
•	Tabasco sauce to taste
1/8	teaspoon cayenne
3/4	cup finely chopped pecans

Combine the cream cheese and Roquefort cheese in a bowl and mix well. Add the celery, onion, Tabasco sauce and cayenne and stir until blended. Shape into a log or ball and roll in the pecans.

Chill, wrapped in waxed paper, until firm.

Yield: 8 servings

Avocado Mango Gazpacho

1 quart Clamato juice
2 cups unsweetened pineapple juice
2 avocados, peeled, chopped
2 tomatoes, seeded, chopped
1 mango, peeled, chopped
1 red bell pepper, chopped
1 green bell pepper, chopped
1 medium red onion, chopped
1/3 cup chopped fresh cilantro
2 teaspoons cumin
• Salt to taste
• Pepper to taste

Combine the Clamato juice, pineapple juice, avocados, tomatoes, mango, bell peppers, onion, cilantro, cumin, salt and pepper in a bowl and mix well.

Chill, covered, for 6 hours. May be stored in the refrigerator for up to 6 days.

Yield: 8 servings

Note: Betty Davis has "doctored" a basic recipe for gazpacho that she saw in the *Boston Globe* by adding the "strange" ingredients of mango, pineapple juice and avocado. This slightly sweet version of gazpacho has won over die-hard "I don't do cold soup, especially gazpacho" haters.

GRAPE GAZPACHO

1/4 cup blanched almonds
2 pounds seedless red grapes
1 to 2 garlic cloves
2 to 3 slices firm white bread, cubed
1 tablespoon olive oil
1 tablespoon wine vinegar
1/2 teaspoon almond extract
• Salt to taste
• Pepper to taste
1/4 cup nonfat plain yogurt

Spread the almonds on a baking sheet. Bake at 350 degrees for 10 minutes or until crisp but not brown. Remove from the oven and let stand until cool.

Purée the almonds, grapes and garlic in a blender. Add the bread, olive oil, vinegar, almond flavoring, salt and pepper and process until smooth. Chill, covered, for 1 hour. Stir in cold water 1 tablespoon at a time if the mixture is too thick. Whisk the yogurt in a small bowl until smooth. Ladle the grape mixture into soup bowls. Place a dollop of yogurt on each serving. Swirl the yogurt into the grape mixture with a knife to marbleize. Serve chilled.

Yield: 4 servings

19

In a sticky mess with your child's sticker collection? Use colorful binders and pages of transparent pockets to hold stickers. Many sticker companies now have special activity paper that fits right into the notebooks.

CONSOMMÉ LYONNAISE

1/4   cup (1/2 stick) butter or margarine
1   pound fresh mushrooms, sliced
2   (15-ounce) cans beef broth
2   broth cans water
1/4   teaspoon nutmeg
1   cup julienned carrots
1/4   cup chopped scallions or
         green onions
3   tablespoons dry sherry

Heat the butter in a saucepan until melted. Add the mushrooms and sauté for 5 minutes. Add the beef broth, water and nutmeg and bring to a boil, stirring frequently.

Add the carrots and simmer for 5 minutes. Stir in the scallions and sherry. Simmer, uncovered, for 1 minute. Serve hot.

Yield: 6 servings

Frustrated with how to display a child's "collection?" From plastic bugs to ballerina figurines, most collections can be displayed on a tiered kitchen spice shelf. Try using the expandable kind since you never know when a new addition will appear.

Italian Bread Salad

1/2 pound 3- to 4-day-old Italian bread

1/2 cup cold water

1 cucumber, peeled, seeded, coarsely chopped

• Salt to taste

5 tablespoons red wine vinegar

2 garlic cloves, minced

1/2 cup extra-virgin olive oil

• Pepper to taste

5 medium tomatoes, seeded, chopped

1 medium red onion, diced

1/2 cup torn fresh basil leaves

Slice the bread into 1-inch-thick slices. Sprinkle the cold water over the bread. Let stand for 2 minutes. Squeeze the bread dry and tear into 1-inch pieces.

Arrange the bread on paper towels and let stand for 20 minutes or until slightly dry. Arrange the cucumber on paper towels and sprinkle with salt. Let stand for 20 minutes. Rinse the cucumber and pat dry.

Whisk the vinegar, garlic and olive oil in a large bowl. Stir in salt and pepper. Add the bread, cucumbers, tomatoes, onion and basil and toss to combine. Let stand for 20 minutes or until the bread has absorbed some of the liquid.

Yield: 8 servings

BROCCOLI SALAD

1   cup mayonnaise
1/3   cup sugar
2   tablespoons wine vinegar
2   large bunches broccoli, finely chopped
3/4   cup Spanish peanuts
3/4   cup raisins
1/2   cup red onion, chopped

Blend the mayonnaise, sugar and vinegar in a small bowl until well mixed. Combine the broccoli, peanuts, raisins and onion in a large bowl.

Pour the mayonnaise mixture over the broccoli mixture, tossing to combine.

Chill, covered, for 2 to 3 hours. May be stored in the refrigerator for 2 to 3 days.

Yield: 8 servings

CABBAGE SLAW WITH PEANUTS

1/4   cup sour cream
1/4   cup mayonnaise
1   teaspoon mustard
1   teaspoon vinegar
1/4   teaspoon salt
1/4   teaspoon curry powder
2   cups finely chopped cabbage
1   bunch green onions, chopped
1   (10-ounce) package frozen green peas, thawed
1/2   cup Spanish peanuts

Blend the sour cream, mayonnaise, mustard, vinegar, salt and curry in a small bowl until well mixed. Combine the cabbage, green onions and peas in a large bowl.

Pour the sour cream mixture over the cabbage mixture, tossing to combine.

Chill, covered, for 2 to 3 hours. Stir in the peanuts just before serving.

Yield: 6 servings

CHINESE CHICKEN SALAD

Chicken:
- Juice of 1 lemon
- 2 tablespoons soy sauce
- 2 garlic cloves, chopped
- Fresh herbs such as chopped cilantro, oregano or parsley to taste
- 4 boneless skinless chicken breasts halves

Dressing:
- 1 cup vegetable oil
- 1/2 cup sugar
- 3/4 cup rice vinegar
- 2 tablespoons sesame oil
- 1 teaspoon salt
- 1 teaspoon pepper

Salad:
- 1 medium head romaine, chopped
- 1 small head Chinese cabbage, shredded
- 4 to 6 scallions, sliced
- 4 ounces sliced almonds
- 3 tablespoons sesame seeds
- 1 (3-ounce) package Chinese ramen noodles, broken and cooked

For the chicken, combine the lemon juice, soy sauce, garlic and herbs of choice in a bowl and mix well. Place the chicken in a glass dish. Pour the marinade over the chicken. Chill, covered, in the refrigerator for 8 to 10 hours. Grill the chicken over hot coals for 8 to 10 minutes on each side or until the juices are clear when the chicken is pierced with a fork. Chop the chicken into bite-size pieces.

For the dressing, combine the vegetable oil, sugar, rice vinegar, sesame oil, salt and pepper in a bowl and mix well. Let stand until the sugar dissolves. May also prepare in a blender.

For the salad, combine the lettuce, cabbage, scallions, almonds, sesame seeds and ramen noodles in a large bowl. Add the chopped grilled chicken and mix well. Whisk the dressing and pour over the salad. Sprinkle with the seasoning from the ramen noodles package, tossing to coat. Chill, covered, until serving time.

Yield: 8 to 10 servings

Coleslaw

8   cups finely shredded cabbage
2   tablespoons sugar
2   tablespoons lemon juice
2   tablespoons mayonnaise
2   tablespoons heavy cream
1/4 teaspoon salt
1/8 teaspoon pepper

Combine the cabbage and sugar in a large bowl and mix well. Chill, covered, for 30 minutes.

Combine the lemon juice, mayonnaise and cream in a bowl and stir until blended. Pour the mayonnaise mixture over the cabbage just before serving, tossing to combine. Sprinkle with the salt and pepper, tossing to coat.

Yield: 20 servings

Cinnamon Salad

1   cup boiling water
1/4 cup red hot cinnamon candies
1   (3-ounce) package cherry gelatin
1   (16-ounce) can unsweetened applesauce

Pour the boiling water over the cinnamon candies in a heatproof bowl, stirring until dissolved.

Add the gelatin and stir until dissolved. Stir in the applesauce. Chill, covered, until set.

Yield: 6 servings

Mandarin Orange Salad

1   (3-ounce) package orange gelatin
3/4 cup boiling water
1   (6-ounce) can frozen orange juice concentrate
1   pint vanilla ice cream, softened
1   cup sliced mandarin oranges

Dissolve the gelatin in the boiling water in a bowl. Add the orange juice, ice cream and mandarin oranges, stirring to combine.

Pour into a 2-quart serving dish. Chill, covered, until set.

Yield: 9 servings

Pineapple Cheese Salad

1   (3-ounce) package lime gelatin
1   (8-ounce) can crushed pineapple, drained
2   cups cottage cheese
1/2 cup chopped pecans

Prepare the gelatin using package directions. Pour into an 8x8-inch dish. Chill until partially set.

Whisk the gelatin lightly until almost frothy. Fold in the pineapple, cottage cheese and pecans. Chill, covered, until set.

Yield: 8 servings

A great storage idea is old suitcases. Keep things such as Legos and drawing supplies in smaller size suitcases. They are quick and easy to grab when you need something for entertainment in the car. Larger suitcases can contain dress-up clothes, car collections and accessories or building blocks.

POTATO SALAD

4 medium potatoes, cooked, cooled
1/2 cup diced celery
1/4 cup diced red onion
1/4 cup parsley
1/4 cup cider vinegar
1/4 cup vegetable oil
1/2 to 1 teaspoon salt
1/4 teaspoon pepper

Peel and dice the potatoes. Combine the potatoes, celery, red onion, parsley, vinegar, oil, salt and pepper in a large bowl and mix well. Let stand for up to 1 hour to blend flavors.

Store, covered, in the refrigerator. May prepare a day in advance.

Yield: 8 servings

An easy way to keep up with children's flash cards—use key rings! Use a hole punch to punch a hole in every flash card. Hold them together with a large key ring (available at hardware stores). This is great for travel because they are not as heavy as books.

Avocado Cheese Dressing

1 avocado, mashed
1 cup cottage cheese
1 tablespoon lemon juice
1/2 teaspoon salt
1/2 teaspoon horseradish
1/4 teaspoon Worcestershire sauce
• Dash of cayenne

Combine the avocado, cottage cheese, lemon juice, salt, horseradish, Worcestershire sauce and cayenne in a bowl and stir to mix well.

Chill, covered, until the flavors are blended. May add a drop of green food coloring if desired.

Yield: 8 servings

Thousand Island Dressing

1 (5-ounce) can evaporated milk, chilled
2 cups mayonnaise-type salad dressing
1 green bell pepper, finely chopped
1 tablespoon pickle relish
1 (12-ounce) bottle chili sauce

Whip the evaporated milk. Add the salad dressing, green pepper, pickle relish and chili sauce and mix well.

Chill, covered, until ready to use. May substitute catsup for the chili sauce. Store in an airtight container in the refrigerator.

Yield: 4 to 4 1/2 cups

Note: This is a "secret" recipe more than 50 years old from the prestigious Rainbow Hotel in Great Falls, Montana.

GREENS, BEANS AND BUNS

VEGETABLES, SIDE DISHES AND BREADS

To get the children to eat their vegetables,

put two piles of veggies on their plate—

one larger than the other.

Then they get to choose which one of

the piles they want to eat. It lets them maintain

the control, and you're ensured that they

are getting their veggies.

Glenda Durst—INA 1993 Nanny of the Year

Apple Cranberry Casserole

3 cups chopped apples
2 cups fresh cranberries
1 1/2 cups sugar
1/2 cup (1 stick) margarine
1 cup rolled oats
1/2 cup packed brown sugar
1/2 cup flour
1/8 teaspoon salt
• Chopped pecans

Combine the apples, cranberries and sugar in a large bowl and mix well. Pour into a greased baking dish. Melt the margarine in a saucepan over medium heat.

Remove from heat and stir in the oats, brown sugar, flour and salt. Stir until well blended. Pour the butter mixture on top of the fruit, spreading well to cover. Top with pecans. Bake at 350 degrees for 1 hour.

Yield: 8 to 10 servings

Note: Delicious served warm with ham.

Baked Apples

4 to 5 medium apples, peeled, sliced
1/2 cup raisins
• Chopped nuts (optional)
1/2 cup water
1/4 cup packed brown sugar
1 tablespoon cornstarch
1 teaspoon vanilla extract
1 tablespoon cinnamon
2 tablespoons (1/4 stick) margarine

Combine the apples, raisins and nuts in a lightly greased 9x13-inch baking dish. Combine the water, brown sugar, cornstarch, vanilla and cinnamon in a bowl and mix well. Pour over the apples and raisins. Dot the top with the margarine.

Bake at 350 degrees for 25 to 30 minutes or until hot and bubbly.

Yield: 6 to 8 servings

BAKED SPICED FRUIT

1   (15-ounce) can sliced peaches, drained
1   (15-ounce) can dark pitted cherries, drained
1   (15-ounce) can pineapple chunks or tidbits, drained
2   oranges, thinly sliced
1   lemon, thinly sliced (optional)
1   cup packed light brown sugar
1/2 teaspoon nutmeg
2   cups sour cream

Combine the peaches, cherries, pineapple, oranges and lemon in a large bowl; mix well. Mix the brown sugar and nutmeg in a small bowl. Arrange the fruit in a greased baking dish in layers, sprinkling each layer with the brown sugar mixture.

Bake at 350 degrees for 30 minutes. Serve warm in individual fruit bowls, topping each serving with sour cream as desired.

Yield: 8 servings

COUNTRY BAKED BEANS

1   pound lean ground beef
2   (16-ounce) cans pork and beans
1   (16-ounce) can kidney beans, drained
1   envelope onion soup mix
1   cup catsup
1/2 cup water
2   tablespoons vinegar

Brown the ground beef in a skillet, stirring until the ground beef is crumbly; drain. Combine the ground beef, pork and beans, kidney beans, soup mix, catsup, water and vinegar in a large bowl; mix well.

Pour into a large baking dish. Bake at 350 degrees for 40 to 45 minutes or until heated through.

Yield: 8 to 10 servings

Hearty Baked Beans

1 pound ground beef
1/2 cup chopped onion
1 (8-ounce) can tomato sauce
1 tablespoon brown sugar
2 tablespoons vinegar
1 teaspoon dry mustard
1 teaspoon salt
1/2 teaspoon thyme
1 (16-ounce) can pork and beans

Brown the ground beef in a skillet, stirring until the ground beef is crumbly; drain. Add the chopped onion and cook until onion is tender. Stir in the tomato sauce, brown sugar, vinegar, dry mustard, salt and thyme.

Let simmer for 10 minutes. Combine the ground beef mixture with the pork and beans in a large baking dish. Bake at 350 degrees for 45 minutes.

Yield: 10 servings

Kahlúa Baked Beans

1 (16-ounce) can pork and beans
1 (16-ounce) can butter beans, drained
1 (16-ounce) can great Northern beans, drained
1 (16-ounce) can kidney beans, drained
1 1/2 tablespoons Kahlúa
• Optional ingredients to taste: bacon, brown sugar, catsup, liquid smoke, mustard, molasses and onion

Combine the pork and beans, butter beans, great Northern beans and kidney beans in a large bowl. Stir in the Kahlúa and desired optional ingredients to taste. Marinate, covered, in the refrigerator for 8 to 12 hours. Pour into a large baking dish and bake at 350 degrees until hot and bubbly.

Yield: 10 servings

Note: May substitute any 4 varieties of beans. May also include any other of your favorite baked bean ingredients.

Cheesy Broccoli Casserole

2   (10-ounce) packages frozen chopped broccoli
1   cup mayonnaise
1   cup shredded sharp Cheddar cheese
2   eggs, lightly beaten
1   cup cream of celery soup
3   tablespoons minced onion
1/2 cup water chestnuts, sliced
•   Tabasco to taste
1   cup seasoned bread stuffing
•   Butter

Cook the broccoli according to the package directions; drain. Combine the broccoli, mayonnaise, cheese, eggs, soup, onion, water chestnuts and Tabasco in a large bowl and mix well.

Pour the mixture into a greased baking dish. Sprinkle the stuffing over the top and dot with butter. Bake at 350 degrees for 45 minutes.

Yield: 8 to 10 servings

Corn Casserole

4   eggs
2   (8-ounce) cans cream-style corn
1   cup shredded Cheddar cheese
1/4 cup (1/2 stick) margarine, melted
1/4 cup flour
1/4 cup sugar
1/8 teaspoon salt
1   green bell pepper, chopped
1/4 cup pimentos

Beat the eggs lightly in a mixer bowl. Stir in the corn, cheese and margarine until well blended. Add the flour, sugar and salt and mix well. Stir in the green pepper and pimentos.

Pour into a greased baking dish. Bake at 350 degrees for 1 hour and 15 minutes.

Yield: 8 servings

CHEESE GRITS

1 cup quick-cooking grits
1 (6-ounce) roll garlic cheese, diced
1/2 cup (1 stick) butter or margarine
1 cup shredded Cheddar cheese

Cook the grits according to the package directions. Add the diced garlic cheese and butter to the hot grits and stir until well blended.

Pour the grits into a 9x13-inch baking dish. Sprinkle the top with the shredded cheese. Bake at 350 degrees for 15 minutes or until hot and bubbly.

Yield: 8 servings

Note: This is great served with chicken, fish or ham.

34

LOW-FAT SPICY FRENCH FRIES

4 medium potatoes
• Artificial butter flakes
• Garlic powder
• Chili powder
• Cumin
• Ground red pepper

Cut the potatoes into thin strips. Arrange on a baking sheet sprayed with non-stick cooking spray. Sprinkle the potatoes with the butter flakes and any combination of spices such as garlic powder, chili powder, cumin and ground red pepper. Place the baking sheet in the middle of the oven.

Bake at 500 degrees for 15 minutes or until golden brown. Remove from oven, turn potato strips and bake for 15 minutes longer or until golden brown.

Serve French fries plain or with catsup or salsa.

Yield: 4 servings

Gourmet Potatoes Supreme

6 to 8 medium potatoes
2 cups shredded Cheddar cheese
2 cups sour cream
$1/2$ cup (1 stick) butter or margarine, melted
$1/2$ cup chopped green onions
• Salt to taste
• Pepper to taste

Combine the unpeeled potatoes and enough water to cover in a large stockpot. Bring water to a boil and cook potatoes until tender and cooked through; drain. Chill the potatoes in the refrigerator until cold.

Grate the unpeeled potatoes coarsely into a large bowl. Combine $1^{1}/2$ cups of the cheese, sour cream, melted butter, green onions, salt and pepper in a bowl and mix well. Stir the cheese mixture into the potatoes.

Spoon into a baking dish and top with the remaining $1/2$ cup cheese. Bake at 350 degrees for 30 minutes or until hot and bubbly.

Yield: 8 servings

Cheesy Potato Casserole

1 (32-ounce) package frozen hash brown potatoes
2 cups sour cream
1 (10-ounce) can cream of chicken soup
3 cups shredded mozzarella cheese
1 cup chopped onion
1 cup shredded Cheddar cheese
2 cups cornflakes
$1/2$ cup (1 stick) butter, melted

Combine the potatoes, sour cream, soup, 2 cups of the mozzarella cheese and onion in a large bowl and mix well. Spread the potato mixture into a greased 9x13-inch baking dish. Sprinkle the remaining 1 cup mozzarella cheese and the Cheddar cheese evenly over the top. Top with the cornflakes and drizzle with the melted butter.

Bake, covered with foil, at 350 degrees for 35 minutes. Uncover and bake for 10 minutes longer or until hot and bubbly.

Yield: 10 to 15 servings

HASH BROWN CASSEROLE

1   (32-ounce) package frozen hash brown potatoes, thawed
2   cups sour cream
1   (10-ounce) can cream of chicken soup
2   cups shredded Cheddar cheese
1/2 cup (1 stick) butter or margarine, melted
1   cup chopped onion
2   teaspoons salt

Combine the potatoes, sour cream, soup, cheese, butter, onion and salt in a large bowl and mix well. Spread the potato mixture evenly into a 9x13-inch baking dish.

Bake at 350 degrees for 45 to 60 minutes or until bubbly and heated through and the top is brown.

Yield: 8 to 10 servings

HASH BROWN QUICHE

3   cups frozen hash brown potatoes, thawed
1/3 cup butter or margarine, melted
1   cup chopped cooked ham
1   cup shredded Cheddar cheese
1/4 cup chopped green bell pepper
1/4 cup chopped onion
2   eggs
1/2 cup milk
1/2 teaspoon salt
1/4 teaspoon pepper

Press the hash brown potatoes over the bottom and up the side of a 9-inch pie plate. Drizzle with the melted butter. Bake at 425 degrees for 25 minutes. Mix the ham, cheese, green pepper and onion in a bowl. Spoon over the potato crust. Beat the eggs, milk, salt and pepper in a small bowl. Pour the egg mixture into the pie plate, covering the ham layer. Bake at 350 degrees for 25 to 30 minutes or until a knife inserted in the center comes out clean. Cool on a wire rack for 10 minutes before serving.

Yield: 4 to 6 servings

Note: This is excellent for breakfast. Add fresh fruit to complete the meal.

POTATO LATKES

6	medium potatoes, peeled
1	small onion
2	eggs, beaten
2	tablespoons flour or matzo meal
1	teaspoon salt
•	Vegetable oil

Rinse and dry the potatoes. Grate the potatoes into a large bowl; drain. Peel the onion. Grate the onion into the large bowl with the potatoes. Add the eggs and mix well. Stir in the flour and salt.

Drop by tablespoonfuls into enough hot oil to barely cover in a large skillet. Cook until golden brown on both sides. Remove from oil to paper towels to drain. Serve warm plain or with applesauce.

Yield: 8 to 10 servings

Note: Children like helping make this Hanukkah treat.

REFRIGERATOR MASHED POTATOES

5	pounds russet potatoes, peeled, quartered
•	Salt to taste
6	ounces cream cheese, softened
1	cup sour cream
2	tablespoons ($1/4$ stick) butter or margarine
2	teaspoons onion salt
1	teaspoon salt
$1/4$	teaspoon pepper

Cook the potatoes in boiling salted water in a saucepan until very tender; drain. Mash the potatoes until smooth in a large mixer bowl. Add the cream cheese, sour cream, butter, onion salt, salt and pepper and beat until smooth and fluffy. Let cool. Spoon into an airtight container and store in the refrigerator. Will keep in the refrigerator up to 2 weeks.

When ready to serve, spoon desired amount into a greased baking dish and dot with butter. Bake at 350 degrees for 30 minutes or until heated through.

Yield: 8 cups

37

Sweet Potato Casserole

3 cups cooked mashed sweet potatoes
1 cup sugar
1/4 cup (1/2 stick) butter or margarine, softened
1/2 cup evaporated milk
1/4 teaspoon salt
3/4 cup packed brown sugar
1/4 cup flour
1/4 cup (1/2 stick) butter or margarine, softened
1 cup pecan halves

Combine the sweet potatoes, sugar, 1/4 cup butter, evaporated milk and salt in a large bowl. Mix until creamy. Spoon the mixture into a buttered 1 1/2-quart baking dish. Combine the brown sugar, flour, 1/4 cup butter and pecans in a bowl and mix until crumbly. Spread the topping evenly over the top of the sweet potatoes. Bake at 350 degrees for 45 minutes.

Yield: 8 to 10 servings

Note: May use canned sweet potatoes, but is better made with fresh sweet potatoes. May also substitute chopped pecans for pecan halves.

Spinach Squares

1/4 cup (1/2 stick) butter
3 eggs, beaten
1 cup flour
1 cup milk
1 teaspoon salt
1 teaspoon baking powder
2 (10-ounce) packages frozen spinach, thawed, drained, patted dry
4 cups shredded Cheddar cheese
1 tablespoon chopped onion
• Seasoned salt to taste

Heat the butter in a 9x13-inch baking dish at 350 degrees until melted. Combine the eggs, flour, milk, salt and baking powder in a large bowl and mix well. Fold in the spinach, cheese and onion. Spoon the spinach mixture into the prepared baking dish and spread evenly. Sprinkle with seasoned salt. Bake at 350 degrees for 35 minutes. Let cool before cutting.

Yield: 10 servings

Note: May substitute a variety of cheeses for the Cheddar cheese or use in combination. May cut into small squares to serve as an appetizer.

ALL-DAY CHEESY MAC

1   (8-ounce) package macaroni
1   cup evaporated milk
3   cups shredded Cheddar cheese
2   eggs, beaten
1½   cups milk
•   Salt to taste
•   Pepper to taste
1   cup shredded Cheddar cheese

Cook the macaroni according to package directions; drain. Combine the macaroni, evaporated milk, 3 cups shredded cheese, eggs, milk, salt and pepper in a large bowl and mix well.

Spoon into a slow cooker sprayed with nonstick cooking spray. Top with 1 cup shredded cheese. Cook on Low for 8 hours. May prepare using low-fat cheese and milk if desired.

Yield: 4 to 6 servings

MACARONI AND CHEESE

16   ounces macaroni
1   (28-ounce) can diced tomatoes
2   (8-ounce) packages Kraft Old English cheese slices

Cook the macaroni according to the package directions; drain. Pour the can of tomatoes into the bottom of a 3-quart baking dish. Cut the cheese into small pieces. Add to the tomatoes and mix well. Pour the hot noodles on top of the tomatoes and cheese and mix well.

Bake at 350 degrees for 45 minutes or until hot and bubbly.

Yield: 12 servings

39

Need a dip for fresh fruit? Try caramel sauce, marshmallow creme or chocolate sauce. Fancy toothpicks also add a new twist to dipping.

OVEN-BUTTERED CORN FINGERS

2¼ cups sifted flour
2 tablespoons sugar
4 teaspoons baking powder
2 teaspoons salt
1 cup cream-style corn
¼ cup milk
⅓ cup butter, melted

Sift the flour, sugar, baking powder and salt into a large bowl. Add the corn and milk and stir until the mixture forms a soft dough. Knead the dough approximately 15 times on a heavily floured surface. The dough will be very moist. Roll into ½-inch thick rectangles and slice into 1-inch "fingers."

Dip into the melted butter and arrange in a 9x13-inch baking dish. Pour the remaining melted butter over the "fingers" in the dish. Bake at 450 degrees for 20 to 30 minutes or until golden brown.

Yield: 24 corn fingers

MEXICAN CORN BREAD

3 eggs, beaten
1 cup milk
1 (8-ounce) can cream-style corn
1½ cups shredded Cheddar cheese
½ cup vegetable oil
1½ cups cornmeal
2 tablespoons flour
1 medium onion, chopped
3 banana peppers, chopped, or 3 tablespoons canned chopped green chiles

Combine the eggs, milk, corn, cheese and oil in a large bowl and mix until well blended. Add the cornmeal and flour and mix well. Fold in the onion and green chiles. Pour into a greased 9x13-inch baking pan. Bake at 375 degrees for 40 minutes. Let cool before cutting.

Yield: 24 servings

Note: Make this corn bread and a big pot of chili to take when going camping. This is how to stay warm on October camping trips.

40

Honey Oat Wheat Bread

2 1/2 cups buttermilk
1/2 cup honey
1/3 cup butter or margarine
3 1/2 cups all-purpose flour
1 1/2 cups rolled oats
2 envelopes dry yeast
2 tablespoons salt
2 eggs
2 1/2 to 3 cups whole wheat flour
• Chopped nuts (optional)
• Raisins (optional)
2 tablespoons (1/4 stick) butter or margarine, melted

Combine the buttermilk, honey and 1/3 cup butter in a saucepan and heat on low until very warm; do not boil. Mix the all-purpose flour, oats, yeast, salt and eggs in a bowl. Pour in the warm buttermilk mixture. Beat on medium speed for 3 minutes. Stir in the whole wheat flour. Fold in the nuts and raisins. Brush the dough with the melted butter. Let rise, covered, in a warm place for 1 hour or until doubled in bulk. Punch down and divide in half. Place into 2 greased 5x9-inch loaf pans. Let rise, covered, in a warm place for 30 to 45 minutes or until doubled in bulk.

Bake at 375 degrees for 25 to 30 minutes or until golden brown. May loosely cover with foil if bread is over browning. Remove to a wire rack to cool.

Yield: 24 servings

Banana Bread

1/2 cup shortening
1 cup sugar
2 eggs, beaten
2 cups flour
1 teaspoon baking soda
3 tablespoons sour cream
2 bananas, mashed
1 cup chopped walnuts

Beat the shortening and sugar in a large mixer bowl until creamy. Add the eggs and beat until light and fluffy. Mix the flour and baking soda together. Add the sour cream alternately with the flour mixture, beating well after each addition. Stir in the bananas and walnuts. Spoon into a greased and floured 5x7-inch loaf pan. Bake at 375 degrees for 1 hour or until loaf tests done. Remove to a wire rack to cool.

Yield: 12 servings

Brown Bread with Raisins

1   cup raisins
1/3 cup water
1   cup sifted all-purpose flour
1 1/2 teaspoons baking soda
3/4 teaspoon salt
1   cup cornmeal
1   cup graham flour
1 1/2 cups milk
1/4 cup molasses
2   tablespoons vegetable oil

Combine the raisins and water in a small saucepan and heat on low until the raisins are plump and tender. Drain and let cool. Sift the all-purpose flour, baking soda and salt into a large bowl. Mix in the cornmeal and graham flour.

Combine the milk, molasses and oil in a small bowl and stir quickly into the flour mixture until well blended. Fold in the raisins. Pour into a greased 4x8-inch loaf pan.

Bake at 350 degrees for 1 hour. Remove to a wire rack to cool.

Yield: 12 servings

Cranberry Nut Bread

1/2 cup (1 stick) butter, softened
1/2 cup sugar
1   egg
2   teaspoons orange zest
2 1/2 cups flour
2 1/2 teaspoons baking powder
3/4 teaspoon salt
1   cup milk
2   cups chopped fresh cranberries
1/2 cup chopped nuts

Combine the butter and sugar in a large mixer bowl and beat until light and fluffy. Beat in the eggs and orange zest. Combine the flour, baking powder and salt in a bowl. Add to the butter mixture alternately with the milk, beating well after each addition. Fold in the cranberries and nuts. Pour the batter into a greased loaf pan.

Bake at 350 degrees for 1 hour. Remove to a wire rack to cool. Let stand for 10 minutes. Invert loaf onto wire rack to cool completely.

Yield: 12 servings

POPPY SEED BREAD

3 cups flour
2¹/₄ cups sugar
1¹/₂ teaspoons salt
1¹/₂ teaspoons baking powder
3 eggs
1¹/₂ cups milk
1 cup plus 2 tablespoons vegetable oil
1¹/₂ teaspoons vanilla extract
1¹/₂ teaspoons almond extract
1¹/₂ teaspoons butter flavoring (optional)
4¹/₂ tablespoons poppy seeds

Combine the flour, sugar, salt and baking powder in a large mixer bowl and mix well. Add the eggs, milk and oil and beat until well blended. Beat in the vanilla, almond extract and butter flavoring. Stir in the poppy seeds.

Pour into 2 greased 5x9-inch loaf pans. Bake at 350 degrees for 1 hour.

Yield: 24 servings

STRAWBERRY BREAD

4 eggs
4 cups sliced strawberries
1¹/₄ cups canola oil
3 cups flour
1¹/₂ teaspoons cinnamon
1 teaspoon salt
1 teaspoon baking soda
1¹/₂ cups chopped pecans

Beat the eggs in a large mixer bowl until fluffy. Mix in the strawberries and canola oil. Combine the flour, cinnamon, salt and baking soda in a bowl. Add to the egg mixture and stir until well blended. Stir in the pecans.

Pour the batter into 2 greased and floured loaf pans. Bake at 325 degrees for 1 hour and 15 minutes.

Yield: 24 servings

43

BEYOND PEANUT BUTTER AND JELLY

MAIN MEALS

To enhance effective communication with the nanny

and the employer, set a time once a month at either

an outside location (restaurant) or at an appointed time

at the employer's office. Make sure child care is set up

beforehand so that is not a factor or an interruption.

Try to limit the amount of notes you leave for your employer.

If you do leave a note, follow up verbally to avoid

any miscommunication.

JANET SCHILLING—INA 1992 NANNY OF THE YEAR

Beef Burgundy with Rice

5 medium onions, thinly sliced
2 tablespoons shortening
2 pounds boneless beef chuck, cut into 1 1/2-inch cubes
1 tablespoon salt
2 tablespoons flour
2 tablespoons pepper
2 tablespoons thyme
2 tablespoons marjoram
1 cup (or more) burgundy or other dry red wine
1/2 cup (or more) beef bouillon
8 ounces fresh mushrooms, sliced
4 cups hot cooked rice

Sauté the onions in some of the shortening in a large skillet. Remove the onions with a slotted spoon to a bowl.

Brown the beef in the remaining shortening in the skillet. Sprinkle with the salt, flour, pepper, thyme and marjoram and mix well. Stir in enough wine and bouillon to cover the beef.

Simmer over low heat for 2 1/2 to 3 hours or until the beef is tender, adding additional wine and bouillon if needed to keep the beef covered. Return the onions to the skillet. Add the mushrooms and mix well. Cook for 30 minutes longer. Serve over the hot cooked rice.

Yield: 6 to 8 servings

HOLIDAY BRISKET WITH VEGETABLES

- 1   center-cut or lean-cut beef brisket
- •   Garlic powder to taste
- •   Oregano to taste
- •   Freshly ground pepper to taste
- 1   envelope instant onion soup mix
- 1   (18-ounce) bottle Open Pit barbecue sauce
- •   Dark brown sugar to taste
- •   Red wine
- 6   carrots, sliced
- 4   potatoes, coarsely chopped
- 4   medium sweet potatoes, coarsely chopped
- 6   ribs celery, sliced

Place the brisket fat side up in a roasting pan. Sprinkle with garlic powder, oregano, pepper and onion soup mix. Pour the barbecue sauce evenly over the brisket. Sprinkle with brown sugar. Add enough wine and water to the roasting pan to surround the brisket.

Bake, covered, at 325 degrees for 45 minutes per pound, basting with the pan juices every $1\frac{1}{2}$ hours. Add the vegetables to the pan juices for the last hour of baking. Remove the brisket to a serving platter. Let stand for 20 minutes before slicing with an electric knife. Serve with the vegetables and serve the pan juices as gravy. May prepare 1 day in advance and may freeze any leftovers.

Yield: variable

Note: This meal has been enjoyed by all Wendy Sachs' friends in every city where she's lived—from Boston to Miami to Philadelphia to New York. It is her signature holiday meal.

BARBECUE BEEF CUPS

3/4   pound ground beef
1/2   cup barbecue sauce
1   tablespoon minced onion
•   Salt and pepper to taste
1   (10-count) can refrigerator biscuits
1/4   cup shredded Cheddar cheese

Brown the ground beef in a skillet, stirring until crumbly; drain. Add the barbecue sauce, onion, salt and pepper. Press each of the biscuits over the bottom and up the side of a muffin cup. Spoon an equal portion of the ground beef mixture into each cup.

Bake at 350 degrees for 10 to 15 minutes or until the biscuits are golden brown and the ground beef mixture is hot and bubbly. Sprinkle with the Cheddar cheese. Bake just until the cheese is melted.

Yield: 10 servings

HAMBURGER NOODLE CASSEROLE

1   pound ground beef
•   Salt and pepper to taste
1   onion, chopped
1 1/2   cups chopped celery
2   cups Cheddar cheese cubes
1   tablespoon Worcestershire sauce
2   cups uncooked wide noodles
1   (4-ounce) can small black olives, drained
1   (14-ounce) can stewed tomatoes
1/4   tomato can water

Brown the ground beef in a large skillet, stirring until crumbly; drain. Season with salt and pepper. Stir in the onion, celery, Cheddar cheese, Worcestershire sauce, noodles and black olives. Pour the tomatoes and water over the top.

Cook, covered, over medium heat for 40 minutes or until the noodles are tender. May substitute the black olive juice for the 1/4 tomato can water.

Yield: 8 servings

Grandmother's Meatballs and Sauce

2 pounds lean ground beef
1/2 pound ground pork
3 eggs, lightly beaten
1 tablespoon Parmesan cheese (optional)
1 teaspoon onion salt
1/2 teaspoon basil
1/2 teaspoon minced garlic
1 cup catsup
1 small onion, finely chopped
1/4 cup packed brown sugar
1/4 cup white vinegar
1/4 cup Worcestershire sauce
1 teaspoon salt
1/8 teaspoon pepper

Combine the ground beef, ground pork, eggs, Parmesan cheese, onion salt, basil and garlic in a large bowl and mix well. Shape into 1- to 2-inch meatballs. Arrange in a baking dish.

Mix the catsup, onion, brown sugar, vinegar, Worcestershire sauce, salt and pepper in a bowl. Pour over the meatballs. Bake at 350 degrees for 45 to 55 minutes or until cooked through. Serve over hot cooked noodles or rice.

Yield: 4 or 5 servings

Note: This may be served as an appetizer or as a buffet item.

*Help children cool off on a hot summer day with water painting.
Give them a bucket of water and clean paintbrushes and ask them to paint the
driveway or sidewalk. The hot sun dries the paintings quickly, so the
little ones will stay busy for hours!*

WORLD'S GREATEST MEAT LOAF

1	egg, lightly beaten
1/4	cup catsup
2	teaspoons prepared mustard
2	teaspoons MSG (optional)
1	teaspoon salt
1/4	teaspoon pepper
1/2	teaspoon basil
1/2	teaspoon thyme
1 1/2	cups soft bread crumbs
2	beef bouillon cubes
3/4	cup boiling water
1/4	cup chopped celery
1/4	cup chopped onion
1	cup shredded Cheddar cheese
2	pounds ground beef

Combine the egg, catsup, mustard, MSG, salt, pepper, basil, thyme and bread crumbs in a large bowl and mix well. Dissolve the bouillon cubes in the boiling water. Add to the egg mixture and mix well. Stir in the celery, onion and Cheddar cheese.

Crumble the ground beef into the bowl and mix lightly and thoroughly. Press lightly into a 5x9-inch loaf pan.

Bake at 375 degrees for 1 hour and 10 minutes.

Yield: 8 servings

To remove gum from hair, try rubbing it with plain peanut butter.
To remove ink from clothing, try hairspray.

Pizza Casserole

2   pounds ground beef
1   medium onion
•   Salt and pepper to taste
1   (16-ounce) package egg noodles
1   (32-ounce) jar spaghetti sauce
1   (16-ounce) jar spaghetti sauce
1   (3-ounce) package sliced
     pepperoni
2   cups shredded Cheddar cheese
4   cups shredded mozzarella cheese

Brown the ground beef with the onion in a skillet, stirring until the ground beef is crumbly; drain. Season with salt and pepper. Cook the egg noodles using the package directions; drain.

Mix the ground beef mixture, egg noodles, spaghetti sauce, pepperoni, Cheddar cheese and 2 cups of the mozzarella cheese in a large bowl. Spoon into three 8x8-inch baking pans. Top with the remaining 2 cups mozzarella cheese.

Bake, covered with foil, at 350 degrees for 30 minutes. Remove the foil. Bake for 30 minutes.

Yield: 18 to 27 servings

Note: This recipe makes a big batch, so freeze some for an easy dinner another night.

Sloppy Joes

1 pound extra-lean ground beef
1 tablespoon vegetable oil
3/4 cup catsup
1 teaspoon prepared mustard
• Salt and pepper to taste
8 hamburger buns

Brown the ground beef in the oil in a skillet, stirring until crumbly; drain.

Add the catsup, mustard, salt and pepper, stirring to mix well.

Simmer until heated through. Serve on hamburger buns.

Yield: 8 servings

Nanny's Sloppy Joes

1 pound ground beef
1/2 cup finely chopped onion
1 cup catsup
1 tablespoon vinegar
1/4 cup packed brown sugar
1 tablespoon prepared mustard
1/2 cup water
1/4 teaspoon paprika
• Hamburger buns

Brown the ground beef with the onion in a skillet, stirring until the ground beef is crumbly; drain. Mix the catsup, vinegar, brown sugar, mustard, water and paprika in a bowl. Add to the ground beef mixture and mix well.

Simmer over low heat for 5 to 10 minutes or until the flavors marry. Serve on hamburger buns.

Yield: 4 to 6 servings

52

Hearty Spaghetti Casserole

1   garlic clove, cut into halves
2   pounds ground beef or turkey
1   large sweet onion, chopped
1   green bell pepper, chopped
3/4   cup olive oil
•   Salt and pepper to taste
1   (8-ounce) can green peas
1   (10-ounce) can whole kernel corn
1   (15-ounce) can tomatoes
1   (2-ounce) jar pimento
1   tablespoon chopped parsley
2   cups pitted black olives
1   (16-ounce) package spaghetti, broken into 1/2-inch pieces
4   cups shredded American cheese

Rub a skillet and a baking dish with the garlic clove. Brown the ground beef with the onion and green pepper in the olive oil in the prepared skillet. Season with salt and pepper. Mix in the peas, corn, tomatoes, pimento, parsley and black olives. Cook the spaghetti in salted water using package directions; drain. Combine the spaghetti and ground beef mixture in the prepared baking dish. Top with the cheese. Bake at 375 degrees for 45 minutes or until bubbly.

Yield: 20 servings

Corned Beef Casserole

12   ounces thin spaghetti, broken into pieces
2   (12-ounce) cans corned beef
1   medium onion, chopped
1   (10-ounce) can cream of chicken soup
1   (10-ounce) can cream of mushroom soup
2   cups milk
2   cups shredded sharp Cheddar cheese

Cook the spaghetti in water to cover in a large saucepan until tender; do not add salt. Drain. Remove all visible fat from the corned beef.

Shred the corned beef into small pieces in a large bowl. Add the onion, soups and milk gradually, mixing well after each addition. Stir in the Cheddar cheese and prepared spaghetti. Spoon into a 9x13-inch baking dish. Bake at 350 degrees for 1 hour.

Yield: 8 to 10 servings

Note: May freeze before baking. Bake frozen casserole for 1 1/4 hours.

Tacos in Pasta Shells

18   jumbo pasta shells
2   tablespoons ($1/4$ stick) butter
$1 1/4$ pounds ground beef
3   ounces cream cheese with chives
1   tablespoon chili powder
$1/4$ teaspoon salt
1   cup taco sauce
1   cup each shredded Cheddar cheese and Monterey Jack cheese
$1 1/2$ cups crushed tortilla chips

Cook the pasta shells in water to cover in a saucepan; drain. Toss with the butter. Brown the ground beef in a skillet, stirring until crumbly. Stir in the cream cheese, chili powder and salt. Simmer for 5 minutes. Spoon into the pasta shells. Arrange in a 9x13-inch baking dish. Pour the taco sauce over the pasta shells.

Bake, covered, at 350 degrees for 15 minutes. Sprinkle with the Cheddar cheese, Monterey Jack cheese and tortilla chips. Bake, uncovered, for 15 minutes longer. Garnish with chopped green onion tops and parsley sprigs.

Yield: 4 to 6 servings

Taco Pizza

1   baked pizza crust
•   Taco sauce to taste
•   Pizza sauce to taste
1   pound ground beef
1   envelope taco seasoning mix
•   Cheddar cheese to taste
•   Mozzarella cheese to taste
•   Chopped lettuce to taste
•   Chopped tomatoes to taste
•   Tortilla chips to taste, coarsely crushed

Place the pizza crust on a pizza pan. Spread with taco sauce and pizza sauce. Prepare the ground beef and taco seasoning mix using the taco seasoning mix directions. Spoon evenly over the pizza crust. Sprinkle with the Cheddar cheese and mozzarella cheese. Bake at 425 degrees for 10 to 15 minutes or until the cheeses are melted. Arrange the lettuce and tomatoes over the top. Sprinkle with the crushed tortilla chips. Serve immediately with additional taco sauce, hot sauce and sour cream.

Yield: 8 servings

Note: May top with black olives and/or chopped onion if desired.

VERSATILE VEGETABLE LASAGNA

2 or 3 (32-ounce) jars spaghetti sauce
1 (16-ounce) package lasagna noodles
• Sliced mushrooms to taste
1 (4-ounce) can sliced black olives, drained
2 (10-ounce) packages frozen spinach, thawed, drained
• Sliced zucchini or other squash to taste
• Fresh tomatoes to taste, cut into quarters
1 (16-ounce) can whole kernel corn, drained
• Low-fat or fat-free cottage cheese or ricotta cheese
4 to 5 cups shredded cheese of choice
• Parmesan cheese to taste

Pour a thin layer of spaghetti sauce over the bottom of an 11x13-inch baking pan sprayed with nonstick cooking spray. Reserve some of the remaining spaghetti sauce and 1/3 of the noodles.

Layer the remaining uncooked noodles, mushrooms, black olives, spinach, zucchini, tomatoes, corn, cottage cheese, remaining spaghetti sauce and shredded cheese 1/2 at a time in the prepared pan. Top with a layer of the reserved noodles and spaghetti sauce.

Bake, covered with foil, at 375 degrees for 2 to 2 1/2 hours or until the noodles are tender. Sprinkle the top with Parmesan cheese. Serve with a green salad and hot Italian bread, or serve with a fruit plate. May include a layer of soy meat, cooked ground beef and/or spicy sausage.

Yield: 8 to 10 servings

Note: This recipe is great to serve for large groups. May freeze individual servings for a quick dinner for one.

Pork Tenderloins with Apples

1   teaspoon cardamom
1   teaspoon cinnamon
1/2 teaspoon pepper
1/4 teaspoon salt
3   or 4 sweet potatoes, peeled, coarsely chopped
1/4 cup olive oil
3   or 4 tart apples, peeled, sliced
2   (12-ounce) pork tenderloins

Mix the cardamom, cinnamon, pepper and salt together. Toss the sweet potatoes in 1/2 of the olive oil and 1/2 of the seasoning mixture in a bowl. Arrange in the bottom of a broiler pan. Bake at 475 degrees for 10 minutes. Add the apples and toss to mix. Push the sweet potatoes and apples to the sides of the pan. Arrange the tenderloins in the center of the pan. Drizzle with the remaining olive oil. Rub with the remaining seasoning mixture. Bake for 10 minutes. Turn the tenderloins over and toss the sweet potatoes and apples. Bake for 10 minutes longer or until the apples are golden brown and the tenderloins are cooked through.

Yield: 4 to 6 servings

Sweet-and-Sour Skillet

1   pound bulk Italian sausage
1   teaspoon oregano
6   cups shredded cabbage
1/3 cup packed light brown sugar
1/3 cup cider vinegar
2   large red apples, sliced

Brown the sausage with the oregano in a skillet over low heat, stirring until crumbly; drain. Stir in the cabbage, brown sugar and vinegar. Bring to a boil. Simmer, covered, for 5 minutes; stir.

Simmer for 5 minutes longer. Arrange the apple slices evenly over the top of the cabbage. Cook, covered, for 2 to 3 minutes or until the apples are tender.

Yield: 4 servings

CHICKEN AND SAUSAGE CASSEROLE

1 whole chicken, cut up
• Salt and pepper to taste
1 pound hot pan sausage
1 cup chopped green bell pepper
1 cup chopped celery
1 small onion, chopped
1 cup sliced mushrooms
1 tablespoon olive oil
1 cup uncooked rice
1 (10-ounce) can cream of mushroom soup
2 envelopes instant chicken noodle soup mix

Place the chicken and water to cover in a large stockpot. Season with salt and pepper. Bring to a boil. Boil for 35 minutes or until the chicken is cooked through and tender. Remove the chicken to a cutting board, reserving 5 cups of the broth. Chop the chicken, discarding the skin and bones.

Brown the sausage in a skillet, stirring until crumbly; drain. Sauté the green pepper, celery, onion and mushrooms in the olive oil in a skillet until tender. Combine the chicken, sausage, sautéed vegetables, rice, soup, soup mix and reserved broth in a large bowl and mix well. Spoon into a large baking dish. Bake at 350 degrees for 1 hour. Serve with a salad and bread.

Yield: 10 servings

To keep a pool cold on hot summer days, use blocks of ice. Take clean, empty milk cartons and plastic soda bottles, fill them with water, and freeze. Cut out the frozen blocks of ice and drop into the pool. Chill out!

CHICKEN AND CHIPS

1 1/2 cups chopped celery
1 1/2 cups sliced fresh mushrooms
3 tablespoons butter
3 cups chopped cooked chicken
1 (10-ounce) can cream of chicken soup
1/2 cup milk
1 cup shredded sharp Cheddar cheese
1 cup sour cream
1 cup mayonnaise
1/2 teaspoon salt
1/2 cup slivered almonds
1 1/2 cups crushed potato chips

Sauté the celery and mushrooms in the butter in a skillet until tender. Combine with the chicken, soup, milk, Cheddar cheese, sour cream, mayonnaise and salt in a bowl and mix well.

Spoon into a 9x13-inch baking dish. Sprinkle with the almonds and potato chips. Bake at 375 degrees for 30 to 35 minutes or until hot and bubbly.

Yield: 6 to 8 servings

CHICKEN SOUFFLÉ

1 (8-ounce) package herb-seasoned stuffing
1/2 cup (1 stick) margarine, melted
1 cup chicken broth
4 cups chopped cooked chicken
1/2 cup each chopped onion and celery
1/2 cup mayonnaise
1/2 teaspoon salt
2 eggs, beaten
1 1/2 cups milk
1 (10-ounce) can cream of mushroom soup
1 cup shredded Cheddar cheese

Combine the stuffing, margarine and broth in a bowl and mix well. Spread half the mixture over the bottom of a greased 9x13-inch baking dish. Spread a mixture of the next 5 ingredients over the stuffing mixture. Top with the remaining stuffing mixture. Pour a mixture of the eggs and milk over the stuffing mixture. Chill, covered, for 8 to 12 hours. Remove from the refrigerator 1 hour before baking. Spread the soup over the top. Bake at 325 degrees for 40 minutes. Sprinkle with the cheese. Bake for 10 minutes or until the cheese is bubbly.

Yield: 10 servings

CHICKEN TORTILLA CASSEROLE

6 whole chicken breasts
2 (10-ounce) cans cream of chicken soup
1 cup sour cream (optional)
2 bunches green onions
1/2 cup (1 stick) butter
1 (4-ounce) can chopped green chiles, drained
1 (8-ounce) can diced water chestnuts, drained
• Salt and pepper to taste
12 corn tortillas
4 cups shredded Monterey Jack cheese

Boil or bake the chicken until cooked through. Chop the chicken coarsely, discarding the skin and bones. Mix the chicken, soup and sour cream in a bowl. Sauté the green onions in the butter until tender. Stir in the green chiles, water chestnuts, salt and pepper. Add to the chicken mixture and mix well. Break the tortillas into pieces.

Arrange a layer of tortilla pieces evenly over the bottom of a baking dish. Layer the chicken mixture alternately with the remaining tortillas, ending with the chicken mixture. Top with the Monterey Jack cheese. Bake at 350 degrees for 30 to 40 minutes or until hot and bubbly. May microwave on High for 15 minutes or until heated through.

Yield: 6 to 8 servings

59

Make a tea party treasure box by decorating an old box with pretty contact paper or wrapping paper. Collect small, old dishes and china. Keep them in your tea party box.

CHICKEN WRAPPERS

3   boneless skinless chicken breasts
1   tablespoon pesto
1½ ounces thinly sliced ham
3   thick slices Cheddar cheese
1   teaspoon butter
2   teaspoons olive oil
2   teaspoons flour
•   Chicken broth to taste
1   tomato, cut into wedges
1   teaspoon sour cream (optional)

Pound the chicken thin between 2 pieces of plastic wrap. Spread 2 of the chicken breasts with the pesto. Arrange equal portions of the ham and cheese over the chicken. Roll to enclose the ham and cheese. Tie with kitchen string.

Cook in the butter and olive oil in a large skillet for 10 minutes or until cooked through and golden brown, turning frequently. Remove the chicken to a plate; keep warm. Add the flour to the pan drippings in the skillet and mix well. Cook for 1 minute. Stir in the desired amount of chicken broth gradually. Bring to a boil, stirring constantly. Cook the sauce until thickened, stirring constantly.

Add the tomato and sour cream. Cook over low heat until heated through, stirring occasionally. Remove the string from the chicken. Arrange the chicken on individual plates and spoon the sauce over the chicken.

Serve with fresh cooked green beans and new potatoes. May serve with additional sour cream if desired.

Yield: 3 servings

Note: To serve to children, you may omit the pesto and slice chicken thinly onto the plate. Depending on the age of the baby, you may want to process the food and sauce to the desired consistency in a food processor. You may chop the food into manageable pieces, omitting the sauce, for older babies.

Grilled Herb Chicken

8 whole chicken breasts
3/4 cup fresh lemon juice
1/4 cup olive oil
1 teaspoon Dijon mustard
4 garlic cloves, crushed
1/4 cup chopped fresh parsley
1 tablespoon chopped fresh rosemary
1 tablespoon each chopped fresh tarragon, sage, oregano and chives
1/2 teaspoon salt
• Freshly ground pepper to taste

Split the chicken breasts. Arrange in a large glass dish. Combine the lemon juice, olive oil, Dijon mustard, garlic, parsley, rosemary, tarragon, sage, oregano, chives, salt and pepper in a bowl and mix well. Pour over the chicken. Marinate, covered, in the refrigerator for 2 hours or longer. Preheat the grill. Remove the chicken, reserving the marinade. Grill the chicken for 20 minutes or until cooked through, turning halfway through the grilling time and brushing frequently with the reserved marinade.

Yield: 8 servings

Note: Use this as a base for chicken sandwiches, adding topping choices such as avocado, salsa, pineapple, bacon, lettuce, tomato and mushrooms. Have a party!

Lemon Chicken

1 egg, beaten
1 pound boneless skinless chicken breasts
3/4 cup bread crumbs
2 tablespoons olive oil
1/2 cup lemon juice
1/2 cup white wine
2 tablespoons (1/4 stick) butter, melted
3 tablespoons sugar

Mix the egg with a small amount of water in a shallow dish. Dip the chicken in the egg and then in the bread crumbs. Brown on both sides in the olive oil in a skillet. Arrange in a baking dish.

Mix the lemon juice, wine, butter and sugar in a bowl. Pour over the chicken. Bake at 350 degrees for 30 minutes.

Yield: 4 servings

PEKING CHICKEN

6   boneless skinless chicken breasts
1   (8-ounce) jar apricot preserves
1   (8-ounce) bottle Russian salad dressing
1   envelope onion soup mix

Arrange the chicken in a 9x13-inch baking dish. Combine the apricot preserves, salad dressing and soup mix in a bowl and mix well. Pour over the chicken.

Bake at 350 degrees for 1 hour or until the chicken is cooked through.

Yield: 6 servings

62

POPPY SEED CHICKEN CASSEROLE

6   to 8 chicken breasts, or 1 whole chicken, cooked
2   (10-ounce) cans cream of chicken soup
1   cup sour cream
1   sleeve butter crackers, crushed
2   teaspoons poppy seeds
3/4   cup (1 1/2 sticks) butter, melted

Cut the chicken into bite-size pieces, discarding the skin and bones. Arrange the chicken in the bottom of a greased 7x11-inch baking dish.

Combine the soup and sour cream in a bowl and spread over the chicken. Sprinkle the crushed crackers and poppy seeds over the soup mixture. Pour the melted butter over the top.

Bake at 350 degrees for 30 minutes or until bubbly.

Yield: 6 servings

ROSEMARY CHICKEN

1/4   cup balsamic vinegar
1/4   cup olive oil
1   tablespoon Dijon mustard
2   garlic cloves, minced
1   tablespoon freshly chopped
      rosemary
•   Freshly ground pepper to taste
4   chicken breasts

Combine the balsamic vinegar, olive oil, mustard, garlic, rosemary and pepper in a glass bowl; mix well. Place the chicken in a plastic resealable bag. Pour the marinade over the chicken and seal the bag. Marinate in the refrigerator for 2 to 10 hours. Place the chicken in a baking dish, discarding the marinade.

Bake at 350 degrees for 35 to 40 minutes or until cooked through. May also grill over medium flame for 6 to 8 minutes on each side.

Yield: 4 servings

Note: This makes a great sandwich with a slice of mozzarella cheese on a hoagie roll.

Recycle crayon stubs. Collect the broken crayons, removing the paper wrappers.
Combine the crayon stubs in an old muffin pan and bake at 300 degrees for 5 to 10 minutes
or until just melted. Let cool and tap on the back of the tin to release.

Pinwheel Turkey Loaf

2   pounds ground turkey
1   cup Italian-seasoned bread crumbs
2   eggs, beaten
$1/2$ cup spaghetti sauce
1   teaspoon Italian herb seasoning
1   (3-ounce) package sliced pepperoni
1   cup Italian-blend shredded cheese
1   (10-ounce) package frozen spinach, thawed, squeezed dry

Combine the ground turkey and the bread crumbs in a bowl and mix well. Add the eggs, $1/4$ cup of the spaghetti sauce and Italian herb seasoning and mix well. Pat the mixture into a 9x13-inch rectangle on waxed paper. Cover the mixture evenly with the pepperoni slices. Top with the shredded cheese and spinach.

Roll the mixture from the 9-inch side into a pinwheel. Place in a loaf pan and top with the remaining $1/4$ cup spaghetti sauce. Bake at 350 degrees for 1 hour. May substitute ground beef for the turkey.

Yield: 6 servings

Turkey Spinach Lasagna

1 pound lean ground turkey
2 (15-ounce) jars spaghetti sauce
1 (6-ounce) can tomato paste
1 (4-ounce) can mushroom stems and pieces, drained
1/2 cup chopped onion
1/2 teaspoon parsley flakes
1/2 teaspoon crushed oregano leaves
1/2 teaspoon crushed basil leaves
1/4 teaspoon garlic powder
• Seasoned salt and pepper to taste
2 cups dry curd cottage cheese
1 cup shredded mozzarella cheese
3/4 cup grated Romano cheese
1 egg, lightly beaten
1 (10-ounce) package frozen chopped spinach, thawed, squeezed dry
8 ounces lasagna noodles, cooked, drained
1 (3-ounce) package pepperoni slices
1/2 cup grated Parmesan cheese
2 cups shredded mozzarella cheese

Brown the ground turkey in a large skillet over medium heat, stirring until crumbly; drain. Stir in the spaghetti sauce, tomato paste, mushrooms, onion, parsley flakes, oregano, basil, garlic powder, salt and pepper. Bring to a boil, stirring constantly; remove from heat. Combine the cottage cheese, 1 cup mozzarella cheese, Romano cheese, egg and spinach in a large bowl and mix well.

Cover the bottom of a 9x13-inch baking dish with 1 1/2 cups of the turkey mixture. Layer with half the noodles and half the cheese mixture. Top with the pepperoni slices. Sprinkle with the Parmesan cheese. Top with the remaining turkey mixture, noodles and cheese mixture in the order listed. Sprinkle with 2 cups mozzarella cheese.

Bake at 350 degrees for 30 to 40 minutes or until bubbly. May broil for 2 to 3 minutes to brown the cheese. Let stand for 10 minutes before serving.

Yield: 8 to 10 servings

A Spoonful of Sugar

Desserts

Life lessons I have learned from my 15 years as a professional nanny—

Keep your word.

Be consistent.

Listen.

Think about what you are saying.

Give lots of hugs.

Mutual respect.

Good communication.

Pick your battles.

Count to 10, or 20 if necessary.

Read.

Learn your limitations and learn to say No!

Stand up for yourself.

Respect other people's feelings, even when you do not agree.

Let go of your anger.

Be forgiving.

Make friends with other nannies.

Some things are not about money.

Get your priorities straight and the rest will fall into place.

Childhood is fleeting; every day is a day we will never get back— make it count.

Ask yourself if it will matter in 5 years.

Leave a legacy.

GLENDA PROPST—INA 1991 NANNY OF THE YEAR

THE BEST BIRTHDAY CAKE

Cake

1   (2-layer) package yellow cake mix
1   (4-ounce) package lemon instant pudding mix
4   eggs
3/4 cup water
3/4 cup vegetable oil

Frosting

1   cup confectioners' sugar
1/3 can frozen orange juice concentrate, thawed
2   tablespoons (1/4 stick) butter, melted

For the cake, combine the cake mix, pudding mix, eggs, water and oil in a large mixer bowl. Beat at medium speed for 5 minutes. Pour the batter into a bundt pan or tube pan. Bake at 350 degrees for 45 minutes.

For the frosting, combine the confectioners' sugar, orange juice concentrate and melted butter in a mixer bowl. Beat at low speed until well blended.

To assemble, invert the cake onto a serving plate. Pierce holes in the top and side of the cake with a fork. Pour the icing over the warm cake. Decorate with birthday cake candles and mint sprigs.

Yield: 16 servings

IDAHO CHOCOLATE CAKE

Cake

1	(4-ounce) russet potato, peeled
2	cups sour cream
1³/₄	cups cake flour
1³/₄	cups sugar
³/₄	cup baking cocoa
¹/₂	cup (1 stick) unsalted butter, softened
2	eggs
1¹/₂	teaspoons baking soda
1	tablespoon vanilla extract
¹/₂	teaspoon salt

Sour Cream Frosting

3	cups confectioners' sugar
¹/₄	cup (¹/₂ stick) butter, softened
3	tablespoons sour cream
1	tablespoon vanilla extract

For the cake, place the potato in a food processor container. Process until shredded. Add half the sour cream, cake flour, sugar, baking cocoa, butter, eggs, baking soda, vanilla and salt to the food processor container with the potato and process for 3 minutes. Transfer the mixture to a large bowl. Process the remaining sour cream, cake flour, sugar, baking cocoa, butter, eggs, baking soda, vanilla and salt for 3 minutes. Add to the potato mixture and mix well. Pour into a greased and floured 9x13-inch cake pan. Bake at 350 degrees for 35 to 40 minutes or until a wooden pick inserted in the center comes out clean. Remove to wire rack to cool.

For the sour cream frosting, combine the confectioners' sugar, butter, sour cream and vanilla in a mixer bowl and beat for 2 minutes or until smooth.

To assemble, invert the cake onto a serving platter and spread frosting over the top and sides of the cake. May spread the frosting over the top of the cake in the pan.

Yield: 15 servings

Jam Cake Dessert

3   cups flour
1   cup sugar
1   tablespoon baking powder
1   cup (2 sticks) butter, softened
1   egg
1   (10-ounce) jar raspberry jam

Combine the flour, sugar and baking powder in a bowl. Place the butter in a large mixer bowl and beat until smooth. Stir in the flour mixture. Make a well in the center of the mixture and drop in the egg. Beat at medium speed until thick and creamy. Reserve 1 cup of the mixture. Spread the remaining mixture in the bottom of a 9-inch pie plate. Spread the jam evenly over the top. Crumble the reserved mixture over the top of the jam. Bake at 350 degrees for 30 to 40 minutes or until the top is golden brown. Let cool before cutting.

Yield: 10 servings

Note: Susan Stimmel's great-aunt Susie was Swiss. She taught Susan this recipe when Susan was a young girl and it is one of her family's favorites.

Pumpkin Dump Cake

1   (30-ounce) can pumpkin pie mix
3   eggs
1   cup evaporated milk
3/4   cup sugar
1   (2-layer) package yellow cake mix
1   cup (2 sticks) butter, melted
•   Chopped pecans

Combine the pumpkin pie mix, eggs, evaporated milk and sugar in a large mixer bowl. Beat at medium speed until well blended. Pour the batter into a 9x13-inch baking pan sprayed with nonstick cooking spray. Sprinkle the cake mix over the batter. Drizzle with the melted butter. Sprinkle with the pecans. Bake at 350 degrees for 60 to 70 minutes or until the cake tests done. Serve with whipped topping.

Yield: 12 to 15 servings

Note: This is a wonderful dessert to serve at a party in the autumn. Garnish each piece with a candy pumpkin or a piece of candy corn.

Easy-Do Fudge

3   cups sugar
3/4   cup (1 1/2 sticks) butter or
       margarine
2/3   cup evaporated milk
2   cups semisweet chocolate chips
2   cups marshmallow creme
1/2   teaspoon vanilla extract
1/2   cup chopped pecans (optional)

Combine the sugar, butter and evaporated milk in a large saucepan. Bring to a boil over medium heat. Cook to 234 to 240 degrees on a candy thermometer, soft-ball stage, stirring constantly.

Remove from the heat and stir in the chocolate chips, marshmallow creme and vanilla until well blended and chocolate chips are melted. Stir in the pecans. Pour into a greased 9x13-inch baking dish. Let cool and cut into squares.

Yield: 3 pounds

Mini Cheesecakes

16   ounces cream cheese, softened
1/2   cup sugar
1   teaspoon vanilla extract
2   eggs
12   vanilla wafers
•   Cheesecake toppings such as
       chopped nuts, chocolate chips,
       bite-size fruit and jam or preserves

Line 12 muffin cups with paper liners. Combine the cream cheese, sugar and vanilla in a large mixer bowl. Beat at medium speed until creamy. Beat in the eggs. Place 1 vanilla wafer in each paper-lined muffin cup. Spoon the cream cheese mixture on top of each vanilla wafer, filling the cups 3/4 full. Bake at 325 degrees for 25 minutes. Remove to a wire rack to cool. Remove from muffin cups when cool and chill in the refrigerator for 30 to 60 minutes. Top each cheesecake with desired topping. Serve immediately.

Yield: 12 mini cheesecakes

Note: Donna Saunders makes these for everything from cookie swaps to school bake sales. She says they are always the first things to be eaten or bought.

Chocolate Oat Cookies

2 cups (4 sticks) butter, softened
2 cups sugar
2 cups packed brown sugar
4 eggs
2 teaspoons vanilla extract
4 cups flour
2 teaspoons baking soda
2 teaspoons baking powder
1 teaspoon salt
5 cups finely ground rolled oats
4 cups chocolate chips
3 cups chopped nuts
1 (8-ounce) chocolate candy bar, grated

Cream the butter, sugar and brown sugar in a large mixer bowl until light and fluffy. Beat in the eggs and vanilla.

Add the flour, baking soda, baking powder and salt and beat well. Stir in the oats until well blended. Fold in the chocolate chips, nuts and grated chocolate bar. Roll into balls and place 2 inches apart on a cookie sheet. Bake at 375 degrees for 10 minutes.

Yield: 9 dozen cookies

Carrot Cookies

1/2 cup shortening
1 cup packed brown sugar
1 teaspoon vanilla extract
1 egg
1 cup cooled mashed cooked carrots
2 cups flour
1/2 teaspoon baking powder
1/8 teaspoon salt
3/4 cup raisins and/or 3/4 cup chopped pecans

Cream the shortening and brown sugar in a large mixer bowl until light and fluffy. Beat in the vanilla, egg and carrots until well blended.

Add the flour, baking powder and salt and beat well. Fold in the raisins and/or chopped pecans.

Drop by spoonfuls onto a cookie sheet. Bake at 375 degrees for 10 minutes or until golden brown.

Yield: about 2 dozen cookies

"To Die For" Chocolate Cookies

1/2 cup dried currants
2 tablespoons Kahlúa
2 ounces baking cocoa
4 ounces bittersweet chocolate
3 tablespoons butter
7 tablespoons flour
1/2 teaspoon freshly ground black
    pepper
1/4 teaspoon baking powder
1/4 teaspoon salt
1/8 teaspoon cinnamon
1/8 teaspoon cayenne
2 eggs, at room temperature
3/4 cup sugar
2 teaspoons vanilla extract
1 cup semisweet chocolate chips

Combine the currants and Kahlúa in a small saucepan. Cook over low heat until warm. Remove from the heat. Combine the baking cocoa, bittersweet chocolate and butter in a small saucepan. Cook over low heat until the butter is melted, stirring frequently. Let cool. Combine the flour, black pepper, baking powder, salt, cinnamon and cayenne in a small bowl and mix well.

Beat the eggs and sugar in a large mixer bowl for 5 minutes or until thick and pale yellow. Stir in the vanilla and melted chocolate mixture. Stir in the flour mixture and mix well. Fold in the currant and Kahlúa mixture and the chocolate chips. The dough will be soft. Drop by spoonfuls onto a cookie sheet lined with parchment paper.

Bake at 350 degrees for 8 to 10 minutes or until the tops are shiny and the cookies are slightly puffed. Let cool for 5 minutes. Remove to wire racks to cool completely. Do not substitute margarine for butter in this recipe.

Yield: 18 cookies

GRAHAM CRACKER SQUARES

Graham Cracker Squares

1	sleeve graham crackers
1	cup (2 sticks) butter
1	cup sugar
1/2	cup milk
1	egg, beaten
1	cup shredded coconut
1	cup chopped nuts
1	cup crushed graham crackers

Frosting

2	cups confectioners' sugar
1/2	cup (1 stick) butter or margarine, softened
1/2	teaspoon vanilla extract
•	Milk or evaporated milk

Assembly

•	Chopped walnuts

74

For the graham cracker squares, grease a 9x13-inch baking pan with butter or shortening. Line the pan with graham cracker squares, reserving some for the top layer. Combine the butter, sugar, milk and egg in a saucepan. Bring to a boil, stirring constantly. Remove from the heat and stir in the coconut, nuts and crushed graham crackers. Pour over the graham crackers in the pan and cover with another layer of graham cracker squares.

For the frosting, combine the confectioners' sugar, butter and vanilla in a mixer bowl and beat until thick and creamy. Add enough milk or evaporated milk to make of the desired spreading consistency.

To assemble, spread the frosting over the graham crackers and sprinkle with chopped walnuts. Chill, covered, for 1 to 2 hours. Cut into 1- to 2-inch squares.

Yield: 20 servings

Mamma's Hamantaschen

Dough

3 1/3 cups flour
1/2 cup sugar
1 1/2 teaspoons baking powder
1/4 teaspoon salt
3 eggs
2/3 cup canola oil
1/4 cup honey
2 tablespoons lemon juice

Filling

1 (10-ounce) jar apricot jam
1/2 cup golden raisins
1/2 cup finely chopped pecans
1/4 cup poppy seeds
1 teaspoon lemon juice

Assembly

1 egg
1 teaspoon water

For the dough, combine the flour, sugar, baking powder and salt in a large bowl. Beat in the eggs, canola oil, honey and lemon juice until well blended. Divide the dough into 3 equal parts. Refrigerate, covered, for at least 1 hour.

For the filling, combine the apricot jam, raisins, pecans, poppy seeds and lemon juice in a bowl and mix well.

To assemble, roll out the dough to a 1/4-inch thickness on a lightly floured surface. Cut out circles with the top of the empty jam jar. Spoon 1/4 to 1/2 teaspoon filling into the center of each dough circle. Bring 3 sides of the dough circle up to the middle with wet fingers. Press to close the top of the pastry. Place on a greased cookie sheet. Beat the egg and water in a bowl. Brush each pastry with the beaten egg mixture. Bake at 350 degrees for 15 minutes or until golden brown.

Yield: 45 pastries

Note: This is a traditional treat eaten during the Jewish holiday of Purim. The pastries are made in the shape of a villain's hat and are eaten in celebration of good winning over evil. This is one of my mother's recipes. Now three generations are enjoying her hamantaschen. Try it if you want to give someone a special treat.

—Bluma K. Marder

HAMANTASCHEN

2 cups (or more) flour
2 teaspoons baking powder
1/2 cup sugar
1/2 cup (1 stick) butter
2 eggs, beaten
1 teaspoon vanilla extract
• Chocolate chips or jam or jelly (any flavor)

Combine the flour, baking powder and sugar in a large bowl. Cut in the butter. Add the eggs and vanilla and mix well. Knead in additional flour if necessary to thicken the dough.

Roll out to a 1/4-inch thickness on a floured surface. Cut into circles with a biscuit cutter. Place a few chocolate chips or 1 teaspoon jam in the center of each circle. Fold up the sides and press the top together to form a triangle. Place pastries on a greased cookie sheet.

Bake at 350 degrees for 30 minutes or until golden brown.

Yield: 2 dozen triangles

LAYER COOKIES

First Layer
1/2 cup shortening
2 eggs, beaten
1 1/2 cups flour
1 cup sugar
1 teaspoon vanilla extract
1 teaspoon baking powder
1/2 teaspoon salt

Second Layer
1 cup packed brown sugar
1 egg white, beaten
1/2 teaspoon vanilla extract
3/4 cup chopped nuts

For the first layer, beat the shortening and eggs in a mixer bowl until light and fluffy. Add the flour, sugar, vanilla, baking powder and salt and beat until well blended. Spread evenly in a 9x13-inch baking dish.

For the second layer, combine the brown sugar, egg white and vanilla in a bowl and mix well. Fold in the chopped nuts. Spread evenly over the first layer. Bake at 350 degrees for 30 minutes. Let cool and cut into small squares to serve.

Yield: 20 servings

Oatmeal Fudge Bars

2   cups packed brown sugar
2   eggs
1   cup (2 sticks) butter, softened
2   teaspoons vanilla extract
2½ cups flour
2   teaspoons salt
1   teaspoon baking soda
3   cups rolled oats
2   cups chocolate chips
1   (14-ounce) can sweetened
    condensed milk
2   teaspoons vanilla extract

Cream the brown sugar, eggs, butter and 2 teaspoons vanilla in a large mixer bowl. Combine the flour, salt and baking soda in a bowl. Beat the flour mixture into the brown sugar mixture until well blended. Stir in the oats. Press 2/3 of the dough into a 10x15-inch baking pan. Combine the remaining ingredients in a saucepan. Cook over low heat until the chocolate chips are melted, stirring constantly. Pour the chocolate mixture over the dough in the pan. Drop the remaining dough by tablespoonfuls over the chocolate layer. Bake at 350 degrees for 25 minutes. Let cool; cut into bars.

Yield: about 2 dozen bars

Peanut Blossoms

½   cup shortening
½   cup packed brown sugar
½   cup sugar
½   cup peanut butter
1   egg
2   tablespoons milk
1   teaspoon vanilla extract
1¾ cups flour
1   teaspoon baking soda
½   teaspoon salt
•   Sugar
48 chocolate candy kisses

Cream the shortening, brown sugar and ½ cup sugar in a large mixer bowl until light and fluffy. Add the peanut butter, egg, milk and vanilla and beat until well blended. Combine the flour, baking soda and salt in a bowl. Add the flour mixture to the peanut butter mixture gradually, beating well after each addition. Shape the dough by teaspoonfuls into balls. Roll the balls in sugar and place on an ungreased cookie sheet. Bake at 375 degrees for 10 to 12 minutes. Top each cookie immediately with a chocolate kiss, pressing firmly.

Yield: 48 cookies

PEANUT BUTTER CUP BARS

2   cups confectioners' sugar
1   cup peanut butter
1   cup (2 sticks) margarine, melted
2/3   cup graham cracker crumbs
1   cup sugar
5   tablespoons margarine
1/4   cup milk
1   cup semisweet chocolate chips

Combine the confectioners' sugar, peanut butter, melted margarine and graham cracker crumbs in a large bowl and mix well. Spread evenly in a 9x13-inch baking pan. Combine the sugar, 5 tablespoons margarine and milk in a saucepan. Bring to a boil and boil for 1 minute.

Remove from the heat. Add the chocolate chips, stirring until melted. Pour over the peanut butter layer. Chill, covered, for 3 hours. Cut into bars to serve.

Yield: 15 to 20 bars

RICE KRISPIE DROPS

1   cup chocolate chips
2   tablespoons peanut butter
4   cups Rice Krispies

Heat the chocolate chips and peanut butter in a saucepan, stirring until the chocolate chips are melted.

Combine the melted chocolate mixture and the cereal in a large bowl, stirring until the cereal is well coated.

Drop by spoonfuls onto a cookie sheet. Chill, covered, for 30 minutes before serving.

Yield: 2 to 3 dozen servings

SPECIAL-K BARS

1   cup light corn syrup
1   cup sugar
1/4   cup (1/2 stick) butter
1   cup peanut butter
8   cups Special-K cereal
1/2   cup chocolate chips
1/2   cup butterscotch chips

Combine the corn syrup, sugar and butter in a large saucepan. Bring to a boil and boil for 1 minute. Remove from the heat and stir in the peanut butter. Combine the peanut butter mixture and cereal in a large bowl. Stir until the cereal is well coated.

Spread in a 9x13-inch baking pan. Melt the chocolate chips and butterscotch chips in a saucepan, stirring constantly. Pour over the cereal layer and spread evenly. Chill, covered, before cutting into bars.

Yield: 15 to 20 bars

Note: Wrap individual bars in plastic wrap for a great lunchtime treat. These appeal to both adults and children.

ZUCCHINI BROWNIES

2   cups sugar
4   eggs
2   teaspoons vanilla extract
1   cup grated zucchini
1   cup shortening
4   ounces baking chocolate
2   cups sifted flour
1   teaspoon baking powder
2   teaspoons salt
1   cup chopped pecans (optional)

Combine the sugar, eggs, vanilla and zucchini in a large mixer bowl and beat until well blended. Melt the shortening and baking chocolate in a large saucepan, stirring constantly. Beat into the sugar mixture.

Combine the flour, baking powder and salt in a bowl. Add the flour mixture gradually, beating well after each addition. Fold in the pecans. Spread in a greased 10x15-inch baking pan.

Bake at 350 degrees for 25 to 30 minutes or until the brownies test done. Let cool before cutting.

Yield: 15 to 20 brownies

FRENCH APPLE TART

Tart

1   cup Grape-Nuts cereal
3   tablespoons frozen apple juice concentrate, thawed
1/2   teaspoon cinnamon
3   medium apples, peeled, cored, thinly sliced
•   Chopped walnuts
2   teaspoons lemon juice

Glaze

1/2   cup water
3   tablespoons apple juice concentrate, thawed
1   tablespoon cornstarch

For the tart, combine the cereal and the apple juice concentrate in a bowl. Let stand until the cereal is softened. Press over the bottom of a buttered 9-inch round cake pan or tart pan. Sprinkle with 1/4 teaspoon of the cinnamon. Arrange the apple slices on top, overlapping slightly. Sprinkle with walnuts. Sprinkle with the lemon juice and remaining 1/4 teaspoon cinnamon. Bake, covered with foil, at 350 degrees for 45 minutes. Let cool.

For the glaze, combine the water, apple juice concentrate and cornstarch in a saucepan. Cook over medium heat until the mixture thickens and turns clear, stirring constantly.

To serve, spoon the glaze evenly over the tart. Chill, covered, until serving time. May top with whipped topping or sour cream.

Yield: 6 to 8 servings

Note: This is an easy, elegant and low-sugar dessert. Joan Friedman says it is best made with apples from the Friedman Family Apple Farm in Dutchess County, New York.

Baked Custard

1   egg, lightly beaten
1   cup milk
3   tablespoons sugar
$3/4$ teaspoon vanilla extract
$1/8$ teaspoon salt
$1/8$ teaspoon nutmeg

Combine the egg, milk, sugar, vanilla and salt in a large bowl and beat well. Pour into two ungreased 6-ounce heatproof custard cups. Sprinkle with the nutmeg.

Place the cups in a baking dish filled with $1/2$ to 1 inch hot water. Bake at 350 degrees for 35 minutes or until set. Serve hot or cold.

Yield: 2 servings

Fruit Pizza

1   (16-ounce) package refrigerator sugar cookie dough
8   ounces cream cheese, softened
8   ounces whipped topping
4   cups assorted sliced fresh fruit such as strawberries, peaches, kiwifruit and bananas
1   cup apple juice or grape juice
1   teaspoon cornstarch

Roll the cookie dough out on an ungreased 16-inch round cookie sheet, spreading to the edge. Bake at 350 degrees for 7 to 10 minutes or until golden brown. Let cool. Beat the cream cheese and whipped topping in a small mixer bowl until creamy. Spread over the cooled cookie crust. Arrange the fruit on top of the cream cheese mixture.

Combine the apple juice and cornstarch in a small saucepan. Bring to a boil and cook until the mixture thickens, stirring constantly. Brush over the fruit to prevent browning and to add shine. Cut into slices and serve immediately.

Yield: 12 to 16 slices

NEBRASKA STRAWBERRY DESSERT

Crust

1   sleeve graham crackers, crushed
1/2   cup sugar
1/4   cup (1/2 stick) butter or margarine, melted

Filling

1   (6-ounce) package strawberry gelatin
12   ounces light cream cheese, softened
16   ounces whipped topping
1   cup confectioners' sugar

Assembly

2   cups fresh strawberries, sliced lengthwise into halves

For the crust, combine the crushed graham crackers, sugar and melted butter in a bowl and mix well. Press over the bottom of a 9x13-inch baking dish. Bake at 350 degrees for 10 minutes. Let cool.

For the filling, prepare the gelatin according to the package directions but using 1 1/2 cups water. Let cool; do not let set. Combine the cream cheese, whipped topping and confectioners' sugar in a large mixer bowl and beat until smooth.

To assemble, spread the cream cheese mixture on the graham cracker crust, smoothing evenly to the edges. Arrange the strawberries on the cream cheese layer. Pour the cooled gelatin over the strawberries. Chill, covered, until set. May serve with additional whipped topping and garnish with sliced strawberries.

Yield: 15 servings

STRAWBERRY PIZZA

1 cup flour
1/2 cup confectioners' sugar
1/2 cup (1 stick) butter, softened
8 ounces cream cheese, softened
1/2 cup sugar
1/2 package junket
1 cup water
2 cups fresh strawberries, sliced

Combine the flour, confectioners' sugar and butter in a mixer bowl and beat until thick and creamy. Spread over the bottom of a 15-inch round cookie sheet. Bake at 325 degrees for 15 minutes. Let cool. Beat the cream cheese and sugar in a mixer bowl until smooth. Spread on the cooled crust. Combine the junket and water in a saucepan. Bring to a boil and boil for 1 minute, stirring constantly. Stir in the strawberries and let cool. Spread on top of the cream cheese mixture. Chill, covered, before serving.

Yield: 8 servings

YOGURT CHEESE PIE

4 cups vanilla yogurt
1 graham cracker crumb pie crust
1 cup fresh blueberries

Spoon the yogurt into a jelly bag or several layers of cheesecloth. Tie the top securely and suspend over the sink or a large bowl. Let the yogurt drain for 6 to 24 hours or until of the consistency of cream cheese.

Spread the yogurt in the graham cracker crust in a pie plate. Top with the blueberries. Chill, covered, before serving.

Yield: 8 servings

Create a surprise when packing an apple for a picnic or lunch. Carve a deep hole in the apple and insert a gummy worm. It is an eye opening treat!

My goal as a nanny is to set a good example.

Most often, children do what you do,

not what you say!

GAIL BITTLE—INA 1995 NANNY OF THE YEAR

ALL-STAR BREAKFAST

2 slices white bread
1 tablespoon butter or margarine
2 eggs
• Salt to taste
• Pepper to taste

Cut a star from the center of each slice of bread using a star-shaped cookie cutter. Reserve bread borders. Toast the stars in a toaster oven.

Melt the butter in a skillet. Place the 2 bread borders in the skillet and cook until lightly brown on both sides. Break 1 egg into the star-shaped hole in each bread border. Sprinkle with salt and pepper. Cook until the eggs are well done, turning once. Serve with the toasted stars.

Yield: 2 servings

86

APPLE BLOSSOM BISCUITS

1   cup wheat Chex cereal
1   medium apple, peeled, grated
$1/2$ cup apple juice
2   cups baking mix
$1/2$ teaspoon cinnamon

Place the cereal in a sealable plastic bag; seal. Press a rolling pin over the bag several times to crush the cereal. Combine the crushed cereal and apple in a bowl. Add the apple juice and mix well. Combine the baking mix and cinnamon in a large bowl. Pour the cereal mixture into the baking mix mixture and stir until well blended.

Drop by spoonfuls onto a greased baking sheet. Bake at 450 degrees for 10 minutes.

Yield: 2 dozen biscuits

Decorate a piece of French toast or pancakes by sprinkling powdered sugar through a lace doily or through a cutout you made with construction paper.

Apple Pizza

Pizza

1	package pizza dough
6	apples, peeled, cored, sliced
1/3	cup sugar
1	teaspoon cinnamon

Topping

3/4	cup flour
3/4	cup sugar
1/4	cup (1/2 stick) butter, melted

For the pizza, roll out the pizza dough to desired thickness. Place on a round baking pan. Arrange the apple slices on the dough. Combine the sugar and cinnamon in a small bowl and mix well. Sprinkle over the apples.

For the topping, combine the flour, sugar and melted butter in a bowl. Mix with hands until the topping is crumbly. Sprinkle the topping over the pizza.

Bake the pizza at 400 degrees for 20 minutes. Cut into slices and serve warm.

Yield: 10 servings

If the kids are too loud in the car, try the "Quiet Game."
The first person to talk is out, the last one to talk is the winner. It's amazing
how long kids can really go without talking!

APPLE SMILES

1   Red Delicious apple, or other red variety
1/4   cup creamy peanut butter
1/4   cup miniature marshmallows

Core the apple and slice into 8 wedges. Spread peanut butter on each apple wedge. Cut the marshmallows in half. Arrange marshmallows in a line on the peanut butter on 4 apple wedges.

Place the other 4 apple wedges on top of the marshmallows, making a sandwich. The apple will look like a mouth with a big smile!

Yield: 4 apple smiles

APPLE STACK SANDWICH

1   medium apple
1   slice American cheese, quartered
1   slice ham or turkey, quartered

Cut the top stem and bottom from the apple; reserve for re-assembly. Core the apple and slice into eight 1/8-inch horizontal slices. Place 1 piece of cheese and ham between every other slice of apple. This will make 4 apple-cheese-ham sandwiches.

Re-assemble the apple on top of the bottom slice and topping with the stem. Wrap tightly in aluminum foil to hold sandwich together securely. This makes a great snack to take traveling or to pack for a picnic or lunch.

Yield: 1 apple sandwich

Banana Split Fruit Salad

1 unpeeled banana
$1/2$ to 1 teaspoon lemon juice
$1/4$ cup fruit cocktail

Peel back one section of the banana. May use a knife to make a neater cut. Remove $1/2$ of the banana using a spoon. Brush the lemon juice onto the exposed part of the banana and banana peel. Spoon the fruit cocktail into the banana. Serve immediately.

Yield: 1 serving

Note: To pack for a picnic or lunch, secure the peel with a wooden pick and wrap tightly in aluminum foil.

Caramel Corn

$1/2$ cup (1 stick) butter
1 cup packed brown sugar
$1/4$ cup light corn syrup
$1/2$ teaspoon baking soda
14 cups air-popped popcorn

Combine the butter, brown sugar and corn syrup in a microwave-safe bowl. Microwave on High for 2 to 3 minutes or until mixture begins to boil; mix well. Stir in the baking soda. Divide the popcorn equally among 4 clean paper bags. Pour the hot caramel mixture over the popcorn. Close the bags securely and shake well to coat. Place 1 bag at a time in the microwave. Microwave on High for 45 seconds. Shake bag vigorously. Spread the popcorn onto waxed paper to cool.

Yield: 14 cups

Note: This is a fun recipe to make with children. They love to help shake the bag and use the air popper. It is a simple and inexpensive gift for children to make and give to teachers and friends. Air-popped popcorn works better than popcorn popped in oil.

COOKIE PAINTING

1   cup (2 sticks) butter, softened
$3/4$ cup sugar
1   egg
$3/4$ teaspoon vanilla extract
$2 3/4$ cups flour
$3/4$ teaspoon baking soda
1   tablespoon water (optional)
•   Variety of colors of food tint
•   Egg yolks

Beat the butter and sugar in a large mixer bowl until creamy. Add the egg and vanilla and beat until light and fluffy. Sift the flour and baking soda into a bowl. Add the flour mixture gradually, beating well after each addition. Divide the dough into 2 equal portions. Add the water if the dough is too crumbly. Cover with plastic wrap and flatten into disks using a rolling pin or your hands. Chill the dough for 1 hour.

Remove the plastic wrap and roll out the dough $1/4$ to $1/2$ inch thick on a lightly floured surface. Cut out six 4x6-inch "canvases." Combine 1 egg yolk and 4 to 5 drops of food tint in a paper cup and mix well. Repeat for every color of food tint. Paint the cookie canvases using the food tint and small, clean paintbrushes. Place 2 canvases on a greased cookie sheet. Bake at 350 degrees for 8 to 10 minutes or until golden brown. Repeat with remaining canvases.

Yield: 6 cookie paintings.

Note: For crisper lines and edges on your artwork, etch an outline of your painting into the canvas with the tip of your paintbrush before painting.

Write a special note and put it into children's lunch boxes. What a nice way to remind a child at school that someone is thinking about them.

CREEPY COOKIE CRITTERS

Grasshopper

2   miniature marshmallows (the eyes)
1   chocolate-covered cream-filled cake roll (the body)
•   Chocolate chips, melted
2   "M&M's" chocolate candies (the eyes)
1   "M&M's" chocolate candy (the nose)
•   Red hot cinnamon candies (the mouth)
1   leaf-shaped spearmint gumdrop (the wings)
•   Green gummy straws (the legs)

Create "eyes" by attaching the marshmallows to the cake with chocolate using a wooden pick; attach "M&M's" to marshmallows. Create "nose" and "mouth" in same manner. Cut the spearmint leaf in half and flatten slightly with a rolling pin. Attach 1 half to either side of cake roll for the "wings" using the melted chocolate or lightly pressing into the cake roll. Attach the "legs" to the bottom of the cake roll using the melted chocolate. Let stand until set.

Yield: 1 creepy cookie grasshopper

Spider

•   Red lace licorice (the legs)
1   chocolate-covered cream-filled round cake (the body)
2   small chocolate-covered mints (the eyes)
2   pieces candy-coated mini chewing gum (the eyes)
1   red jellybean (the nose)
•   Chocolate chips, melted
•   Peanut butter candy sprinkles

Stick the licorice into the round cake using a wooden pick to help make holes. Create "eyes" and "nose" by attaching candy to cake with melted chocolate using a wooden pick. Press the sprinkles over the body.

Yield: 1 creepy cookie spider

Note: Creepy critter cookies can be made to resemble lizards, beetles, ants and snakes. Try experimenting using different cookies and candy. Legs are usually made out of lace licorice and eyes out of small round candies. The bodies can be made out of sandwich cookies or round cream-filled cakes.

FUDGE POPS

1 (4-ounce) package chocolate pudding and pie filling mix
3 cups milk
1/4 cup sugar
1/2 cup whipping cream, whipped

Combine the pudding mix, milk and sugar in a saucepan and mix well. Bring to a boil over medium heat. Cook for 2 minutes, stirring constantly. Let cool for 30 minutes, stirring occasionally.

Fold in the whipped cream. Pour into small paper cups or popsicle molds. Freeze until partially frozen and insert wooden sticks or plastic spoons in the center of each pop. Freeze for 3 to 4 hours or until firm.

Yield: 13 fudge pops

EASY GRILLED CHEESE SANDWICH

2 slices bread (any variety)
1 or 2 slices cheese (any variety)

Toast the bread slices in the oven or toaster oven. Place cheese on 1 slice of the toasted bread. Cover with the other slice of bread. Place on a microwave-safe plate.

Microwave on High for 10 to 20 seconds or just until cheese begins to melt. Let stand until cool.

Yield: 1 sandwich

93

Make sandwiches with flair! Use your cookie cutters to make them fun to eat. How about a Christmas tree in July?

ICE CREAM SANDWICH

2 large, soft cookies (any variety)
• Peanut butter
• Candy sprinkles
1 scoop ice cream (any variety)
• Jelly (optional)

Cut a star out of 1 of the cookies using a small star-shaped cookie cutter. Discard the small star-shaped cookie. Spread a small amount of peanut butter on both cookies and sprinkle with the candy sprinkles. The cookie with the star cutout will be the top to the ice cream sandwich.

Place the scoop of ice cream on the bottom cookie. Top the ice cream with the cookie with the star cutout. Press lightly to flatten slightly.

May add a small amount of jelly to the center of the cookie inside the star-shaped cutout. Serve immediately or wrap in foil and freeze.

Yield: 1 ice cream sandwich

Hate to have all those tub toys cluttering up the tub? Children love to play with measuring cups that can be thrown in the dishwasher for easy cleanup.

I Scream for Witches

12   scoops green mint chocolate chip
      ice cream
12   chocolate ice cream cones
12   chocolate wafer cookies
1/2   cup chocolate chips, melted
•   Red lace licorice
•   Mini baking "M&M's"
•   Candy sprinkles
12   bugle-shaped crispy corn snacks
•   Shredded wheat cereal
12   cream-filled cupcakes

Freeze the scoops of ice cream on a baking sheet. Attach the ice cream cones to the chocolate wafers using the melted chocolate chips. These will be the hats. Let stand until set.

Tie the licorice around the hats. Remove the ice cream from the freezer. Create "eyes" by pressing "M&M's" and sprinkles onto the ice cream. Press a hat onto the top of each scoop of ice cream. Press a bugle-shaped corn snack on the ice cream for the "nose." Attach a small amount of shredded wheat cereal to the sides of the scoops of ice cream for "hair," pressing firmly.

Return the decorated ice cream to the freezer until ready to serve. Place each witch on top of a cupcake and serve immediately.

Yield: 12 witches

1,2,3 Peanut Butter Cookies

1   cup peanut butter (creamy or crunchy)
1   egg, beaten
1   cup sugar

Combine the peanut butter, egg and sugar in a large bowl and mix well. Shape the dough into balls. Place 2 inches apart on a cookie sheet. Flatten the balls using a fork.

Bake at 350 degrees for 5 to 8 minutes or until crispy around the edges. Remove to wire rack to cool.

Yield: 1 dozen cookies

Note: For best results, use a natural peanut butter without added sugar. If the dough appears too sticky, add a small amount of flour to stiffen.

Mini Pizzas

1   (6-count) package English muffins
1   (14-ounce) jar pizza sauce
•   Chopped cooked meats, such as pepperoni, Canadian bacon and sausage
•   Shredded cheese (any variety)

Split each muffin in half. Spread the pizza sauce evenly onto each muffin half. Add the desired meat toppings. Sprinkle with desired amount of shredded cheese. Place muffins onto a baking sheet.

Bake at 400 degrees for 8 to 10 minutes or until cheese is melted and bubbly. Let cool for 1 to 2 minutes.

May also add a variety of other toppings such as: sliced olives, chopped onion and peppers, sliced mushrooms or pineapple.

Yield: 12 muffin halves

Note: If serving to a group, let the children create their own pizza.

POPCORN TREATS

10   cups popped popcorn
1   (16-ounce) can salted peanuts, finely chopped
1   (10-ounce) package small gumdrops
1/2 cup (1 stick) margarine
1   (24-ounce) package miniature marshmallows

Combine the popcorn, peanuts and gumdrops in a large bowl. Melt the margarine in a large saucepan over medium heat. Add the marshmallows and stir until melted. Pour the hot marshmallow mixture over the popcorn mixture and mix until well coated.

Press the mixture into a greased 9x13-inch dish using buttered hands. Let stand until firm. Cut into squares to serve.

Yield: 15 to 20 servings

Note: This is easy and fun for preschoolers to help make and eat.

Keep a jar of spare change by the door for the last minute "I need lunch money" syndrome. An old Equal jar with a flip-top lid works great for quickly pouring out change.

PRETZELS

2 teaspoons dry yeast
1 1/2 cups warm water
3/4 teaspoon salt
1/2 teaspoon honey
4 cups flour
1 egg, lightly beaten
• Salt (optional)

Dissolve the yeast in the water in a bowl. Stir in 3/4 teaspoon salt and honey. Add the flour and mix well using a wooden spoon. Do not let the dough rise. Place the dough on a floured surface and knead for 5 minutes or until the dough is soft and smooth. Divide the dough into small balls (about the size of a golf ball). Roll each ball into thin ropes. Shape the ropes into the desired shapes, such as pretzel braids or alphabet shapes.

Arrange on a lightly floured baking sheet. Brush the pretzels with the egg and sprinkle with salt. Bake at 400 degrees for 10 to 20 minutes depending on the thickness of the pretzel. Remove to a wire rack to cool.

Yield: 3 to 6 dozen pretzels

Note: This recipe comes out of our book, *Playtime, A Guide to Children's Creative Play.* Copyright 1996 Helping Hands (A division of the Childcare Connexion). Written by Joan Ferriter Ross and illustrated by Heidi Pietrzak Hupal.

—Helping Hands,
Child Care Placement Service

STRESS-RELIEVER COOKIES

3   cups rolled oats
1½   cups packed brown sugar
1½   cups flour
1½   cups (3 sticks) butter, softened
1½   teaspoons baking powder

Combine the oats, brown sugar, flour, butter and baking powder in a large bowl. Mix and knead the batter using hands until thoroughly blended. Roll into small balls and place on a cookie sheet. Bake at 350 degrees for 10 to 12 minutes or until golden brown.

Yield: 2 to 3 dozen cookies

Note: This is a great recipe to use to release children's tension on bad winter weather days. It helps to ease the "cabin fever."

If children are afraid of monsters at bedtime, use monster spray (room deodorizer) to scare them away!

MAKE A WISH

BIRTHDAY THEME PARTIES

Take the time to take care of yourself.

We often forget when we are so busy taking care

of others. It is important to have a life and outside interests

other than your job. Get involved in outside activities and

be your own person. This will make you a happier person,

more energetic, able to give more to your family,

and makes your time special!

CYNTHIA WILKINSON—INA 1998 NANNY OF THE YEAR

CHEESE CRISP BEACH BALLS

2 cups shredded sharp Cheddar cheese
1 cup (2 sticks) margarine, softened
2 cups flour
2 cups crisp rice cereal

Combine the cheese and margarine in a large mixer bowl and beat until well blended. Add the flour and mix well. Fold in the cereal gradually. Shape the mixture into small balls and place on an ungreased cookie sheet. Flatten each ball with a fork. Bake at 375 degrees for 10 minutes.

Yield: 3 dozen

STRAWBERRY AND MELON SALAD

Dressing
1/4 cup orange juice
1 envelope Italian-style dressing mix
1/2 cup vegetable oil
2 tablespoons water

Salad
1 (10-ounce) package mixed salad greens
3 cups melon balls or cubes
1 cup sliced strawberries
3 tablespoons sunflower seeds

For the dressing, pour the orange juice into a glass jar with a tight-fitting lid. Add the dressing mix, oil and water. Replace the lid and shake vigorously until well blended.

For the salad, combine the salad greens, melon and strawberries in a large bowl. Pour the dressing over the salad, tossing well to coat. Sprinkle with the sunflower seeds just before serving.

Yield: 12 servings

BACKYARD PIZZA-JOES

1 pound ground beef
1 (14-ounce) jar pizza sauce
2 cups shredded mozzarella cheese
4 hamburger buns

Brown the ground beef in a skillet, stirring until crumbly; drain. Stir in the pizza sauce and cheese. Simmer, covered, until heated through and cheese is melted. Serve on buns.

Yield: 4 sandwiches

Note: This is a great picnic sandwich. Wrap immediately in foil and place in an ice chest to keep warm.

GREAT IDEA!

Send invitations cut out of construction paper in the shape of sunglasses, swimming pools, or inner tubes. Don't forget to include that guests should bring a swimsuit, sunscreen, and beach toys.

BANANA SPLIT DESSERT

2 cups graham cracker crumbs
1/2 cup (1 stick) butter or margarine, melted
1/4 cup sugar
2 cups confectioners' sugar
2 egg whites
1/2 cup (1 stick) butter or margarine, softened
4 bananas, sliced
1 (20-ounce) can crushed pineapple, drained
16 ounces whipped topping
1 large package crushed pecans
1 (6-ounce) jar maraschino cherries

Mix the first 3 ingredients in a large bowl. Press mixture over the bottom of a 9x13-inch dish. Combine the confectioners' sugar, egg whites and softened butter in a large mixer bowl. Beat at medium speed for 10 minutes. Spread over the graham cracker crust. Top with the bananas, pineapple and whipped topping. Sprinkle with the pecans. Cut into squares. Top each square with a maraschino cherry. Chill, covered, until serving time.

Yield: 12 to 15 servings

103

PURPLE FRUIT AND MILK PASSION

1/4 cup frozen grape juice concentrate
2   tablespoons milk

Combine the grape juice concentrate and milk in a blender container. Process until smooth. Pour immediately into a chilled insulated container with an airtight lid. Chill until serving time. Refrigerate any remaining drink.

Yield: 1 serving.

Note: One-fourth cup of frozen fruit juice concentrate is equal in nutritional value to 1 cup of fruit. This is an easy way to get important nutrients in a fun drink that kids will adore.

JEWEL CRACKERS

30   butter crackers
3/4 cup creamy peanut butter
3/4 cup grape or strawberry jelly

Spoon the peanut butter into a decorator tube fitted with a star tip. Pipe the peanut butter around the edge of each cracker. Spoon a small amount of the jelly in the center of each cracker. Serve immediately. May substitute cream cheese for the peanut butter for guests who are allergic to peanuts.

Yield: 30 crackers

GREAT IDEA!

Party favors for the Cinderella party can include anything with a Cinderella theme, such as sticker books or coloring books with crayons.

Purchase clear plastic slippers and fill with candy for each guest.

BIPPITY-BOPPITY-BOO FRUIT KABOBS

30   wooden skewers
•   Marshmallows
•   Assorted fruit, such as apple slices,
      banana slices, cantaloupe balls,
      honeydew balls, maraschino
      cherries and pineapple chunks

Arrange marshmallows and fruit in
serving platters and serve buffet-style.
Allow guests to create their own fruit
kabobs by sliding marshmallows and
fruit onto the skewers.

Yield: 30 kabobs

DECORATED JUICE BOXES

•   Juice boxes of choice
•   Aluminum foil
•   Assorted colors plastic wrap
•   Assorted colors curling ribbon

Cover each juice box with foil, leaving
room for the straw. Cover foil with
colored plastic wrap, gather excess at
top of box and tie with curling ribbon.
Punch the straw in the box and tie
curling ribbon on the straw.

Yield: variable

105

MELON CHICKEN SALAD

1/4 cup plain nonfat or reduced-fat yogurt
1/4 cup reduced-fat mayonnaise
1   tablespoon fresh-squeezed lemon juice
1   tablespoon chopped fresh chives
1/4 teaspoon salt
5   cups cantaloupe cubes
2 1/2 cups shredded cooked chicken
1   cup green grape halves
1   cucumber, peeled, quartered lengthwise, thinly sliced

Combine the yogurt, mayonnaise, lemon juice, chives and salt in a bowl and whisk until well blended. Add the cantaloupe, chicken, grapes and cucumber and stir until well coated. Serve on a bed of lettuce.

Yield: 4 servings

Note: This is an easy and healthy meal to serve kids on a hot day or at an outdoor party. Buy a chicken already cooked from your local deli for a real time-saver.

MAGIC WANDS

- Newspaper
- Tape
- Aluminum foil
- Gold or silver poster board
- Assorted colors curling ribbon

Roll 3 sheets of newspaper and wrap well with tape to make the wand handle. Trim the edge to make it even. Cover the handle with foil and secure with tape.

Cut 2 stars out of poster board. Cut several long pieces of curling ribbon. Pull each ribbon across the blade of a pair of scissors to curl the ribbon. Glue one end of each ribbon to the bottom of 1 of the stars. Glue the other star on top of the side with the ribbon glued to it, leaving a small opening at the bottom.

Insert the handle in the small opening of the star, securing with a small amount of glue. Let the wand dry.

106

CHEESY PASTA AND BACON

6   ounces pasta
2/3   cup shredded four-cheese blend cheese
2/3   cup nonfat ricotta cheese
3   ounces Canadian bacon, chopped
1/8   teaspoon pepper

Cook pasta using the package directions. Drain and return to the saucepan. Combine the shredded cheese and ricotta cheese in a and mix well. Stir into the pasta. Add the Canadian bacon and pepper; toss to combine. Cook for 2 minutes or until the cheese is melted.

Yield: 6 servings

Note: Experiment using different types of pasta in this recipe. Try macaroni noodles, shells or bow-tie pasta. Try different combinations of cheese, too. The possibilities for this dish are endless!

GREAT IDEA!

Purchase Cinderella paper party products, or if not available use pretty metallic foil paperware.

Purchase a Cinderella cake or make your own by using a doll cake pan.

Make "Jello Jigglers" with different flavors of gelatin using heart- or jewel-shaped candy molds.

Play musical crowns instead of musical chairs using the Cinderella soundtrack and a toy gold crown.

107

Pass out plastic construction hats to all the guests. Adult helpers can wear fluorescent vests and tool belts.

FROZEN EARTHWORM POPS

1   (4-ounce) package pistachio
    instant pudding mix
1   (4-ounce) package chocolate
    instant pudding mix
24 gummy worms
12 popsicle molds or
    12 small paper cups
12 wooden sticks

Prepare the pudding mixes according to package directions. Let stand for 5 minutes. Spoon the pistachio pudding into the molds, filling the molds halfway. Place 2 gummy worms in each mold. Spoon the chocolate pudding over the top. Insert a wooden stick halfway in each mold. Freeze for 4 hours or until frozen. Remove from molds to serve.

Yield: 12 pops

Cake and Cookie Dirt

2   (3-ounce) packages chocolate
    instant pudding mix
2   prepared (8-inch) round chocolate
    cakes
3   to 4 cups chocolate cookie crumbs

Prepare the pudding mix according to package directions. Cut each cake into 6 approximately equal portions. Place each portion into clean, small toy dump trucks. Top the cake with the pudding and cookie crumbs. Serve with small plastic toy shovels. It is a dessert and a take-home party favor all in one!

Yield: 12 servings

GREAT IDEA!

Create streamers from red danger tape and yellow construction tape purchased from a hardware store. Tie yellow, white and black balloons everywhere.

Use orange construction netting and create a maze for the guests to walk through. Add some orange construction barrels and cones if possible.

109

GREAT IDEA!

Decorate your backyard to look like the Hundred Acre Woods where Pooh and all his friends live. Create Winnie-the-Pooh characters on poster board and place around the yard.

Order a "beehive cake" from the bakery. Ask them if they could include bees made out of frosting with paper wings and honeycomb decorations. You could also serve cupcakes with a bee on top.

For a party game, play pin the tail on Eeyore. Make a giant Eeyore and several tails out of poster board. If it starts to rain on the party, go inside and watch "Winnie-the Pooh" movies.

POOH'S HONEY GRAHAM TREATS

35   Keebler honey graham crackers
$1/2$ cup (1 stick) butter
$1/2$ cup sugar
•   Slivered almonds to taste

Arrange the graham crackers close together on a cookie sheet. Melt the butter in a saucepan over medium heat. Stir in the sugar. Bring to a boil. Boil for 2 minutes, stirring constantly. Pour the butter mixture over the graham crackers. Sprinkle with almonds. Bake at 350 degrees for 10 minutes. Remove with a spatula to waxed paper to cool. Separate into squares. Store in an airtight container.

Yield: 35 graham treats

RABBIT'S
CARROT CAKE

Cake

1 (2-layer) package carrot cake mix
1 cup sour cream
2 carrots, shredded
1/2 cup raisins
1/2 cup finely chopped pecans

Cream Cheese Frosting

1 (1-pound) package confectioners'
   sugar
1/2 cup (1 stick) butter, softened
12 ounces cream cheese, softened
1 teaspoon vanilla extract

For the cake, prepare the cake mix according to the package directions, adding the sour cream and stirring in the carrots, raisins and pecans. Pour into a 9x13-inch cake pan. Bake according to the package directions or until the cake tests done.

For the frosting, combine the confectioners' sugar, butter, cream cheese and vanilla in a large mixer bowl. Beat at medium speed until smooth.

Spread the Cream Cheese Frosting over the cake. Chill until serving time.

Yield: 15 servings

111

FISH BAIT

12	gummy worms
12	blue gummy sharks
24	(6-inch) strips red shoestring licorice
1	cup oyster crackers
1	cup fish-shaped pretzel crackers
1	cup fish-shaped cheese crackers

Combine the gummy worms, gummy sharks, licorice, oyster crackers and fish crackers in a large bowl and toss well. Serve from a large plastic bucket, which may also serve as a table centerpiece. May also divide evenly into individual small plastic buckets or goody bags and give as party favors.

Yield: 5 cups

OCEAN FISHWICHES

8	frozen fish fillets
8	curly lettuce leaves
8	hamburger buns
1	large carrot
1	red bell pepper
16	large black olive slices
16	frozen green peas, thawed

Bake the fish fillets according to the package directions. Place a lettuce leaf on the bottom half of each hamburger bun. Place a fish fillet on top of each lettuce leaf. Cut the carrot into 1 1/2-inch pieces. Cut each piece lengthwise into 2 rectangle-shaped slices. Cut each rectangle into 2 triangle-shaped slices. Place 1 carrot triangle on each side of the fish fillet, allowing them to protrude from the fish fillet to resemble fins.

Cut 8 small triangles out of the red pepper and press into the front of each fish fillet to resemble a mouth. Place two olive slices above the mouth to make the eyes. Place a pea in the center of each olive slice. Cover each sandwich partially with the top half of the hamburger bun, leaving the face exposed.

Yield: 8 fishwiches

113

SEASHELL PASTA

4   ounces medium pasta shells
4   ounces dark green rotelle
1   red bell pepper
1/2 cup prepared Italian salad
     dressing
1/4 cup sliced pimento-stuffed green
     olives

Bring a generous amount of water to a boil in a large saucepan. Add the shells to the boiling water and cook for 7 minutes. Add the rotelle to the boiling water and cook for 7 minutes longer or until both pastas are tender. Drain the pastas, rinse with cold water and drain again. Slice the red pepper into 4 large pieces. Cut into as many shapes as possible using 1-inch cookie cutters. Combine the pastas, red pepper shapes, dressing and olives in a large bowl and toss well to coat. Chill, covered, until serving time. Toss again immediately before serving.

Yield: 8 servings

GREAT IDEA!

Cut out large fish placemats from construction paper. Let each child have a different fish.

Show the movie "The Little Mermaid" or play the sound-track from the movie.

STARFISH PIZZA

8   slices firm white bread
8   slices mozzarella cheese
1/4 cup pizza sauce
•   Black olives, sliced

Cut each slice of bread into a star shape using a 3-inch star-shaped cookie cutter. Cut each slice of cheese into a star shape using a 2-inch star-shaped cookie cutter. Arrange the bread on a large baking sheet. Broil for 1 to 2 minutes, turning once. Spread a small amount of the pizza sauce on top of the toasted bread. Place a star-shaped piece of cheese on top of the pizza sauce. Create eyes and a smiling mouth on top of the cheese using the olive slices. Broil for 2 to 3 minutes or until the cheese is melted.

Yield: 8 pizzas

GREAT IDEA!

Hand out bandanas and eye patches as each guest arrives at the party or ask everyone to come dressed as a pirate.

Set up a treasure hunt. Divide children into 2 groups and give them a map to follow to the hidden treasure. Have a big treasure chest filled with party goodies at the end of the hunt.

PIRATE BROCCOLI BREAD

3   eggs
8   ounces low-fat small curd cottage cheese
1/4   cup (1/2 stick) butter or margarine, melted
1/8   teaspoon hot pepper sauce
1   (10-ounce) package frozen chopped broccoli, thawed
2   (7-ounce) packages corn muffin mix
1/2   cup chopped onion
1   cup shredded Swiss cheese
2   tablespoons grated Parmesan cheese

Combine the eggs, cottage cheese, butter and hot pepper sauce in a large mixer bowl and beat until smooth. Add the broccoli, corn muffin mix, onion, Swiss cheese and Parmesan cheese and mix well. Spoon into a greased 9x13-inch baking dish. Bake at 375 degrees for 30 minutes or until golden brown and a wooden pick inserted near the center comes out clean. Cut into bars to serve.

Yield: 12 to 15 servings

WALK THE PLANK SHEET CAKE

Cake

2	cups flour
2	cups sugar
1/2	teaspoon salt
2	eggs, beaten
1/2	cup sour cream
1	teaspoon baking soda
1	teaspoon vanilla extract
1	cup (2 sticks) margarine
1	cup water
1/4	cup baking cocoa

Chocolate Frosting

1/2	cup (1 stick) margarine
1/4	cup baking cocoa
2	tablespoons milk
1	(1-pound) package confectioners' sugar

For the cake, combine the flour, sugar and salt in a large mixer bowl and mix well. Add the eggs, sour cream, baking soda and vanilla and beat until smooth. Combine the margarine, water and baking cocoa in a saucepan over medium heat. Bring to a boil. Add to the batter and mix until smooth. Spoon into a greased 10x15-inch baking pan. Bake at 350 degrees for 20 minutes or until the cake tests done.

For the frosting, melt the margarine in a saucepan over medium heat. Stir in the baking cocoa and milk. Bring to a boil. Remove from the heat. Add the confectioners' sugar and mix well.

Spread the frosting over the warm cake.

Yield: 15 to 20 servings

117

PEOPLE PUPPY CHOW

1   cup chocolate chips
1/2   cup (1 stick) butter
2/3   cup creamy peanut butter
1   (18-ounce) box Crispix cereal
3   cups confectioners' sugar

Place the chocolate chips in a microwave-safe bowl. Microwave on High until melted, stirring frequently. Combine the butter and peanut butter in a microwave-safe bowl. Microwave until melted, stirring frequently. Pour the melted butter mixture in the melted chocolate and stir until well blended. Pour the chocolate mixture over the cereal in a large bowl and mix well to coat. Spoon 1 1/2 cups of the confectioners' sugar into a clean paper bag. Spoon half the cereal mixture into the paper bag, close bag and shake well to coat cereal. Pour coated cereal mixture into a large airtight container. Repeat with the remaining confectioners' sugar and cereal mixture. Store in an airtight container.

Yield: 10 cups

118

GREAT IDEA!

Play party games such as "Pin the Tail on the Puppy," or instead of "Duck, Duck, Goose," play "Dog, Dog, Cat."

Use clean plastic dog bowls to eat out of or to fill them with party favors.

DOGGIE BONES

2 cups flour
2 teaspoons baking powder
1/2 teaspoon salt
1/2 cup shortening
2/3 cup shredded Cheddar cheese
1/2 cup finely chopped ham, bologna
   or salami
3/4 cup milk

Combine the flour, baking powder and salt in a medium bowl. Cut in the shortening until crumbly. Add the cheese and ham and mix well. Pour in the milk, stirring until a soft dough forms. Knead gently 10 times on a lightly floured surface. Pat the dough into an 8-inch square. Cut the square into halves. Cut each half crosswise into 1x4-inch strips. Arrange the strips on an ungreased baking sheet. Bake at 450 degrees for 12 to 15 minutes. Serve warm or at room temperature. May serve with catsup, mustard or cheese dip.

Yield: 16 doggie bones

120

PUP CAKES

1 (2-layer) package any flavor cake mix
1 (16-ounce) can any flavor white frosting
   Chocolate chips
24 chocolate mint wafers

Prepare cake mix according to package directions for 24 cupcakes. Remove to a wire rack to cool. Allow each child to frost his or her cupcake using a plastic knife or small spatula. Allow each child to decorate his or her own "Pup Cake" by placing a wafer in the middle of the cupcake and 3 or 4 chocolate chips in a semi-circle above the wafer to resemble a paw print.

Yield: 2 dozen cupcakes

Note: Celebrate a "Bear Party" with these cakes. Ask everyone to bring their favorite stuffed bear to the party and call these cupcakes "cub cakes."

PAPER PLATE PUPPY MASK

- Scissors
- Paper plates
- Assorted colors construction paper
- Glue

Cut two holes for eyes out of the paper plate. Cut ears, mouths, spots and noses out of different colors of construction paper. Glue onto the paper plate. Let children use their creativity to create his or her own individual puppy.

PLAY "CHASE THE DOG" GAME

- Children (as many as are present at the party)
- Bandanas
- Basketballs

Tuck the bandanas into each child's back pocket, belt loop or elastic waistband to resemble a tail. Designate an area for the game to take place. The players must continually dribble their ball and stay within the designated area, while trying to retrieve other players' bandanas. When a player loses his "tail," he is out of the game and must sit down outside the designated area. The game continues until only 1 player is left with a tail. That player is "top dog."

121

FESTIVE HOLIDAYS

HOLIDAY PARTIES

Allow the parents to have their own family time

with the nanny present. This will allow for bonding

within the family without competition from the nanny.

It will help distinguish the family and nanny times

but still leave the nanny as part of the family.

HEIDI KUEHNER—INA 1999 NANNY OF THE YEAR

HUGS-AND-KISSES COOKIES

Cookies
1 (18-ounce) package refrigerator sugar cookie dough

Butter Cream Frosting
1¼ cups sifted confectioners' sugar
½ cup (1 stick) butter, softened
½ teaspoon vanilla extract
1 to 2 tablespoons milk

• Tinted sugar (variety of colors)

For the cookies, roll out the dough to a ¼-inch thickness on a lightly floured surface. Cut the dough into large Xs and Os using a cookie cutter or a knife. Place the cookies on a lightly greased cookie sheet and bake according to the package directions. Remove to a wire rack to cool.

For the frosting, combine the confectioners' sugar, butter and vanilla in a mixer bowl and beat until creamy. Beat in the milk gradually until the mixture is of spreading consistency. Spread the cookies with the butter cream frosting and sprinkle with the tinted sugar.

Yield: 2 to 3 dozen cookies

124

GREAT IDEA!

Add finely chopped red maraschino cherries to your favorite sugar cookie recipe. Cut out the cookies with heart-shaped cookie cutters and you have a delightful Valentine's Day treat.

STRAWBERRY SURPRISE MUFFINS

6   tablespoons (3/4 stick) butter,
       softened
3/4   cup sugar
2   eggs
1/2   cup milk
14   fresh strawberries, mashed
2   cups flour
1/4   teaspoon salt
1   tablespoon baking powder
12   chocolate or white chocolate
       candy kisses or 2 tablespoons
       strawberry jam

Combine the butter and sugar in a large mixer bowl and beat until creamy. Beat in the eggs and milk gradually. Stir in the strawberries and mix well. Sift the flour, salt and baking powder into a bowl and mix well. Add the flour mixture to the strawberry batter, stirring until well blended. Fill paper-lined muffin cups 1/2 full. Place a candy kiss or 1/2 teaspoon of strawberry jam in each muffin cup. Top with batter until each cup is almost full. Bake at 350 degrees for 20 to 25 minutes or until the muffins begin to brown and a wooden pick inserted near the centers comes out clean. For a Valentine's Day delight, use valentine-decorated paper liners.

Yield: 12 muffins

GREAT IDEA!

Decorate Valentine goodies bags with heart-shaped sponges dipped in paint.

CANDY LOLLIPOPS

8   ounces assorted red, pink and/or
      clear hard candies
•   Assorted small decorative candies
      such as red hot cinnamon candies,
      small nonpareils, small colored
      candy hearts, spice drops and
      gumdrops
•   Lollipop sticks

Place unwrapped hard candies in a large plastic sealable bag. Place the plastic bag on top of a folded towel and crush candies with a meat mallet or small hammer. Place four 2$\frac{1}{2}$- to 3$\frac{1}{2}$-inch round or heart-shaped metal cookie cutters on a baking sheet lined with foil. Spoon approximately 2 tablespoons of the crushed candy into each cookie cutter. Add the small decorative candies.

Bake at 350 degrees for 6 to 8 minutes or until the candies are completely melted. Cool for 30 seconds. Remove cookie cutters with tongs, allowing the melted candy to spread slightly. Attach a stick to the base of each lollipop immediately. May press more decorative candy into the hot lollipops if desired. Let cool and peel the foil from the bottom of each lollipop. Repeat the process.

Yield: 8 lollipops

Note: These lollipops are not intended for small children.

126

STRAWBERRY SALAD

1   (6-ounce) package strawberry
     gelatin
1½   cups boiling water
1   (10-ounce) package frozen
     sweetened strawberries, thawed
1   (8-ounce) can crushed pineapple
1   cup sour cream

Dissolve the gelatin in the boiling
water, stirring constantly. Stir in the
strawberries and undrained pineapple.
Drain the fruit, reserving the liquid.
Reserve 1 cup of the liquid and let stand
at room temperature. Pour the fruit and
the remaining liquid into a 5-cup mold
or 9-inch square pan coated with
nonstick cooking spray. Chill, covered,
for 1 hour or until set. Whisk the sour
cream and the reserved liquid in a
bowl. Pour over the top of the salad.
Chill, covered, until set. Unmold onto
a serving plate or cut into squares to
serve. Garnish with leaf lettuce and
strawberries.

Yield: 8 servings

GREAT IDEA!

Make a mobile with different
size hearts cut from colorful
construction paper. Punch holes
in the top of each heart and
hang with yarn of different
lengths tied to a coat hanger.

Fold and cut red construction
paper to make a string of
hearts. Write love messages
with a marker on each heart.

Make valentine place mats for
your entire family. Cut
construction paper to the
desired shape and size of the
place mats. Decorate the place
mats using stickers, doilies,
photographs, and other various
decorative items. Laminate the
place mats and enjoy during
the Valentine holiday.

Make valentines for friends and
family using pictures cut out of
magazines and old greeting
cards. Use the pictures to create
secret messages, or use symbols
and pictures in place of words.
Use your creativity!

127

Shamrock Garlic Bread

1   loaf Italian bread
1/4   cup (1/2 stick) butter, softened
1/4   cup chopped parsley
2   garlic cloves, minced

Slice the bread into halves lengthwise. Cut the bread with a shamrock-shaped cookie cutter of desired size. Combine the butter, parsley and garlic in a bowl and mix until blended. Spread the butter mixture on each slice of shamrock bread. Place the bread on a baking sheet and bake at 400 degrees for 12 to 15 minutes or until golden brown.

Yield: variable

Green Salad

- Any variety of salad greens such as iceberg lettuce, romaine lettuce or fresh spinach leaves
- A variety of green vegetables such as cucumber, celery, green bell pepper, snow peas, avocado and sprouts
- Salad dressing

Chop the lettuce and desired green vegetables into bite-size pieces. Combine the lettuce and vegetables in a large bowl and toss to mix well. Serve with your favorite prepared salad dressing.

Yield: variable

128

PESTO PASTA

1 pound spinach fettuccini or linguini
1 1/2 cups packed fresh basil leaves
1/2 cup chopped walnuts
2 garlic cloves, chopped
2/3 cup olive oil
2/3 cup grated Parmesan cheese
1/4 teaspoon salt
1/4 teaspoon pepper

Cook the pasta according to the package directions; drain and keep warm. Place the basil leaves in a food processor container and process until coarsely chopped. Add the walnuts and garlic and process until finely ground. Add the olive oil in a fine stream, processing constantly until smooth. Add the cheese, salt and pepper and process until mixed. Combine the pasta and pesto in a large serving bowl and toss to coat. May serve with additional Parmesan cheese if desired.

Yield: 4 to 6 servings

GREAT IDEA!

Go on a leprechaun hunt! Leave a trail of green footprints cut out of construction paper that lead to a "Pot of Gold." The pot can contain treats such as chocolates covered with gold foil, coins, or goldfish crackers.

129

LIME SHERBET WITH FRUIT

- Lime sherbet
- Topping suggestions: honeydew melon balls, kiwifruit slices, mint leaves, mint chocolate wafer cookies, lime slices, mint chocolate chips

Scoop the lime sherbet into individual dessert dishes. Top with a variety of toppings.

Yield: variable

SHAMROCK SHAKE

- Vanilla ice cream
- 2 cups milk
- Mint-flavor syrup to taste

Fill a blender container half full with ice cream. Add the milk and mint syrup to the ice cream and process until smooth. Add enough mint syrup to achieve the desired amount of green.

Yield: 2 servings

COFFEE FILTER SHAMROCKS

- Coffee filters
- Green food coloring
- Water

Cut out different sizes of shamrocks from the coffee filters. Combine the desired amount of food coloring with water in a small bowl. Fold the paper shamrocks and dip slowly into the tinted water. The longer the shamrock is immersed, the more color it will absorb. Remove from the bowl, unfold the shamrock and let dry. You can punch small holes in the tops of the shamrocks and string onto yarn, making a string of shamrocks to hang. Or glue onto construction paper and make St. Patrick's Day cards for family and friends. Experiment with the shamrocks and the many festive ways in which to use them!

GREAT IDEA!

Search for four-leaf clovers! Irish legend says that good luck will come to anyone who finds one, so get hunting!

POT-OF-GOLD PAINTED BREAD

- Food coloring (variety of colors)
- $1/4$ cup milk for each food coloring
- Firm white bread slices

Combine 1 to 2 drops of food coloring with $1/4$ cup milk in a small bowl. Repeat the process for each color used. Paint a rainbow and a pot of gold on each slice of bread with a clean cotton swab using the food coloring mixtures. Toast the bread slices in a toaster oven until golden brown. Serve warm with butter.

Yield: variable

131

Make Rice Krispie Treats using Kellogg's Razzle Dazzle Rice Krispies. Let the mixture cool slightly and shape into 3-inch eggs. These make yummy Easter eggs.

Make a jelly bean trail for children to follow that leads to their Easter basket. Give them a small basket in which to gather their jelly beans as they follow the path the Easter Bunny left for them.

132

BUNNY BISCUITS

1   (10-count) can refrigerator biscuits
•   Raisins
1/4   cup (1/2 stick) melted butter
•   Sugar (optional)

Show children how to separate the biscuits. Give each child two biscuits and allow them to cut 1 into halves with a plastic knife. Attach the 2 biscuit halves to either side of the remaining whole biscuit to form the bunny ears. Let the children decorate the bunny face using raisins to make eyes, a nose and a mouth. Brush with melted butter and sprinkle with sugar. Bake using the package directions.

Yield: 5 bunny biscuits

Hot Cross Bunnies

3¹/₂ to 4 cups flour
2   packages active dry yeast
1   teaspoon cinnamon
³/₄   cup milk
¹/₂   cup vegetable oil
¹/₃   cup sugar
³/₄   teaspoon salt
3   eggs
²/₃   cup dried currants
1   egg white, lightly beaten
1¹/₂ cups sifted confectioners' sugar
¹/₄   teaspoon vanilla extract
¹/₈   teaspoon salt
•   Milk

Combine 1¹/₂ cups of the flour, yeast and cinnamon in a large bowl; mix well. Combine the milk, oil, sugar and ³/₄ teaspoon salt in a saucepan and cook just until warm, stirring constantly. Add the milk mixture to the flour mixture. Add the eggs and beat at low speed for 30 seconds, scraping the side of the bowl constantly. Beat at high speed for 3 minutes. Stir in the currants and enough of the remaining flour to make a soft dough. Knead on a lightly floured surface for 3 to 5 minutes or until smooth and elastic. Shape into a ball. Place in a greased bowl, turning to coat. Let rise, covered, in a warm place until doubled in bulk. Punch the dough down and turn out onto a lightly floured surface. Cover and let rest for 10 minutes. Divide into pieces. Roll some of the dough in long thin pieces to form a bunny body and head. Cut some of the dough and shape to form the ears and tail. Attach the ears and tail with wooden picks. Repeat the process until all the dough is used. Place 1¹/₂ inches apart on a lightly greased baking sheet. Cover and let rise for 30 to 40 minutes or until almost doubled in bulk. Brush the tops of the bunnies with the egg white, reserving a small amount. Bake at 375 degrees for 12 to 15 minutes or until golden brown. Let cool slightly and remove the wooden picks. Combine the confectioners' sugar, vanilla, ¹/₈ teaspoon salt and reserved beaten egg white in a mixer bowl. Beat until blended, adding enough milk for the desired consistency. Ice the bunnies with the confectioners' sugar glaze.

Yield: variable

134

EASTER SUGAR COOKIES

2¼ cups sugar
1 cup shortening
2 teaspoons vanilla extract
2 eggs
6 cups flour
1 teaspoon salt
2 teaspoons baking soda
1 cup sour cream
• Cinnamon
• Tinted sugar

Combine the sugar, shortening and vanilla in a large mixer bowl and beat until light and fluffy. Beat in the eggs. Sift the flour, salt and baking soda into a large bowl. Add to the sugar mixture gradually, beating well after each addition. Beat in the sour cream. Chill the dough, covered. Roll ⅛ inch thick on a floured surface. Cut out cookies using Easter-theme cookie cutter shapes such as bunnies, eggs and chicks. Sprinkle with cinnamon and tinted sugar. Bake at 350 degrees for 8 to 9 minutes or until golden brown.

Yield: 2 dozen cookies

CRUNCHY EASTER BASKETS

2   cups butterscotch chips
1   (12-ounce) package chow mein
    noodles
•   Jelly beans

Microwave the butterscotch chips in a microwave-safe bowl on High until melted, stirring at 15-second intervals. Pour the melted butterscotch chips over the noodles in a large bowl, tossing with a wooden spoon until well coated. Let cool slightly. Shape by hand into $1/4$-cup stacks and place on a cookie sheet or waxed paper. Make a small indention in the middle of the stack. Let cool completely. Fill stacks with jelly beans.

Yield: 2 dozen crunchy baskets

Note: May use chocolate chips for Wood Stacks or white chocolate chips for Birch Stacks.

135

APPLE PIE PANCAKES

1   egg
3/4   to 1 cup milk or buttermilk
1   cup whole wheat flour
1   tablespoon sugar
1   teaspoon baking powder
1   teaspoon baking soda
1/2   teaspoon salt
1   teaspoon cinnamon
1/2   teaspoon nutmeg
1   medium apple, peeled, cored, chopped
2   tablespoons vegetable oil

Beat the egg in a bowl until fluffy. Add the milk and mix well. Beat in the whole wheat flour, sugar, baking powder, baking soda, salt, cinnamon and nutmeg. Fold in the apple. Spread the oil on a hot griddle. Pour about 1/4 cup batter at a time on the hot griddle for each pancake. Bake until bubbles appear on the surface and the underside is golden brown. Turn the pancake over. Bake until golden brown.

Yield: 6 to 8 medium pancakes

DAIRY-FREE BANANA MUFFINS

1   cup sugar
1/4   cup (1/2 stick) milk-free margarine, softened
1   or 2 eggs
1   cup mashed ripe banana
1   cup oat bran
3/4   teaspoon baking soda
1/2   teaspoon salt

Cream the sugar and margarine in a mixer bowl until light and fluffy. Add the egg and beat well. Stir in the banana. Sift the oat bran, baking soda and salt together. Add to the banana mixture and mix well. Pour into 12 greased or paper-lined muffin cups. Bake at 350 degrees for 25 to 30 minutes.

Yield: 12 muffins

136

EGGS-IN-A-POCKET

2	tablespoons (1/4 stick) butter or margarine
1/4	cup chopped green bell pepper
1	small tomato, seeded, chopped
8	large eggs
1	teaspoon Worcestershire sauce
1/4	teaspoon salt
2	pita rounds, cut into halves
1/4	cup shredded Cheddar cheese

Melt the butter in a 10-inch skillet over medium heat. Sauté the green pepper in the butter for 3 minutes or until tender. Add the tomato and cook for 1 minute. Combine the eggs, Worcestershire sauce and salt in a mixer bowl and beat until light and fluffy. Add to the hot skillet. Cook for 3 to 5 minutes or until the eggs are cooked through, gently lifting the outside edge with a spatula and tilting the skillet as they cook. Spoon the egg mixture into the pita halves and sprinkle with the cheese.

Yield: 4 eggs-in-a-pocket

137

GREAT IDEA!

Make a poster sign that reads "Mom is Wow upside down." Take pictures of each child holding the sign and then give the pictures to Mom.

GINGERBREAD PANCAKES WITH MAPLE WHIPPED CREAM

Maple Whipped Cream
1 1/2   cups whipping cream
1/2   cup maple syrup

Pancakes
4   cups buttermilk pancake mix
1   tablespoon cinnamon
1   tablespoon ground ginger
2 1/3   cups water
1/2   cup molasses

For the whipped cream, combine the whipping cream and maple syrup in a mixer bowl and beat until soft peaks form. Chill, covered, for 2 hours before serving.

For the pancakes, combine the pancake mix, cinnamon and ginger in a large bowl and mix well. Add the water and molasses, stirring just until moistened. Pour 3 tablespoons at a time onto a hot lightly greased griddle or skillet. Bake for 4 to 5 minutes or until golden brown, turning once.

To serve, top pancakes with maple whipped cream.

Yield: 12 pancakes

Note: Pancakes may be frozen for up to 3 months. Place frozen pancakes directly on the oven rack and bake at 350 degrees for 5 minutes or until heated through.

GREAT IDEA!

Make Mom a special sunshine T-shirt. Draw a circle on the shirt with yellow fabric paint. Let the child dip a hand in the paint and make a border around the circle, fingers facing outward to create sun rays. Below the sun write "You are my Sunshine." The child may paint a face on the sun, too.

138

MOM'S COFFEE CAKE

GREAT IDEA!

3/4   cup sugar
1/2   cup shortening
1   teaspoon vanilla extract
3   eggs
2   cups flour
1   teaspoon baking powder
1   teaspoon baking soda
1   cup sour cream
6   tablespoons (3/4 stick) butter, softened
1   cup packed brown sugar
2   teaspoons cinnamon

Several weeks before Mother's Day have children start writing down things about their mother for which they are thankful, such as: "Mom made my lunch," "Mom read me a bedtime story," or "Mom makes the best Macaroni and Cheese." Place the slips of paper in a decorated jar or painted shoebox for the children to give on Mother's Day. It will be a gift that will make Mom cry!

Combine the sugar, shortening and vanilla in a large mixer bowl and beat until creamy. Beat in the eggs 1 at a time. Sift the flour, baking powder and baking soda in a large bowl. Add half the flour mixture to the sugar mixture and mix well. Add the sour cream and beat until well blended. Add the remaining flour mixture and mix well. For the topping, combine the butter, brown sugar and cinnamon in a bowl and mix well. Pour half the batter into a greased and lined 10-inch tube pan. Sprinkle with half the topping mixture. Pour the remaining batter into the pan and top with the remaining topping mixture. Bake at 350 degrees for 50 minutes or until the coffee cake tests done. Cool on a wire rack before inverting.

Yield: 16 servings

WILD WEST BAKED BEANS

1/2   pound bacon, chopped, crisp-fried, drained
1/2   pound lean ground beef, cooked, drained
1   (28-ounce) can baked beans
1   (16-ounce) can butter beans
1   (16-ounce) can kidney beans
1   small white onion, chopped
1/2   cup packed brown sugar
1/2   cup sugar
1/4   cup catsup
2   tablespoons molasses
2   tablespoons prepared mustard

Combine the bacon, ground beef, baked beans, butter beans, kidney beans, onion, brown sugar, sugar, catsup, molasses and mustard in a large bowl and mix well. Spoon into a greased 9x13-inch baking dish. Bake at 350 degrees for 1 hour.

Yield: 8 servings

BOURBON MUSTARD MARINADE

1   cup water
1   cup soy sauce
1/4   cup bourbon
1/4   cup plus 2 tablespoons packed brown sugar
1   tablespoon dry mustard
3   garlic cloves

Combine the water, soy sauce, bourbon, brown sugar, dry mustard and garlic in a bowl and mix well. Pour over chicken or pork in a shallow dish. Marinate, covered, in the refrigerator for several hours or for up to 2 days.

Yield: 2 1/4 cups

Note: May combine the marinade and pork chops in a plastic resealable bag and freeze. The pork will marinate as it thaws in the refrigerator.

140

DAD'S FAVORITE THINGS

- Scissors
- 3 sheets of different colored construction paper
- 1 (8x11-inch) acrylic frame
- Glue sticks
- Photo of children
- Marker
- Stickers
- Pictures cut out of magazines that reflect Dad's life, interests and "favorite things"

Cut 1 sheet of construction paper to fit into the frame. Cut the remaining 2 sheets of construction paper to form mattes for the frame and glue together as desired. Glue the photo to the center of the mattes. Write "Dad's Favorite" with the marker on the paper above the picture. Attach desired stickers around the picture. Glue various pictures from magazines around the picture. Let dry completely. Slide the picture into the frame.

Yield: 1 frame

Take pictures of the children dressed up in Dad's shirts and ties or work uniform, such as a doctor's coat. Let them hold Dad's briefcase, doctor's bag, or whatever Dad might take to work. They will look so cute dressed in clothes that hang down to their toes and the poses and outfits make such memorable photos.

141

CHIP OFF THE OLD BLOCK

- Glue
- Photo of child
- 1 (5- to 6-inch-long) piece of 2x4 wood
- Clear wood varnish

Glue the photo of the child on 1 side of the piece of wood. Write with a permanent marker or wood burn the words, "Chip Off the Old Block" above the photo. Let dry. Varnish the piece of wood and photo with clear varnish. This makes a great Father's Day gift for fathers or grandfathers.

142

THROW A BACKYARD
BAR-B-QUE FOR DAD

Decorate your backyard with a picnic and ant theme. Make giant ants out of black construction paper and set them on the table and place them around the backyard.

Make a sheet cake with white frosting. Decorate it with black decorator icing to look like a grill and place on it 2 plastic steak doggie toys.

Decorate the entire backyard with red and white balloons.

Sprinkle small, black plastic ants all over the table like confetti.

Serve Wild West Baked Beans and grilled pork chops or chicken with Bourbon Mustard Marinade (page 140).

Create a watermelon fruit basket. Help Mom carve the watermelon to look like a pretty basket and fill it with a variety of fun fruits such as watermelon chunks, cantaloupe and honeydew melon balls, grapes, strawberries and blueberries. This makes a beautiful centerpiece on the picnic table!

The picnic would not be complete without Ants on a Log. Fill celery sticks with creamy peanut butter and top with raisins for a favorite snack of adults and kids alike.

143

Use pumpkins that have been cleaned out as vases for fresh flowers. You can also use gourds and squash as candle holders. Use different sizes, and experiment using them as votive holders. Cut small holes in the sides and let the glow of the candle show through.

GHOST POTATOES

1 recipe mashed potatoes
• Black beans, cooked

Spoon the mashed potatoes into a pastry bag fitted with a decorator tip. Pipe onto plates in shapes to resemble ghosts. Place 2 black beans on each mashed potato ghost to resemble eyes.

Yield: variable

Note: If you do not have a pastry bag, use a resealable plastic bag with 1 corner cut off.

STUFFED PUMPKINS

4 small pumpkins
2 (15-ounce) cans black beans, rinsed and drained
2 (16-ounce) cans whole kernel corn, drained

Wash and dry the pumpkins. Place the pumpkins on a baking sheet. Bake at 350 degrees for 30 minutes. Cut off the top of the pumpkins and scoop out the seeds. Cook the beans and corn according to can directions. Combine the cooked beans and corn in a bowl and mix well. Spoon the warm beans and corn into the baked pumpkins. Serve immediately for a festive and colorful Halloween treat.

Yield: 4 stuffed pumpkins

BOO CUPS

3½ cups cold milk
2 (4-ounce) packages chocolate instant pudding mix
16 ounces whipped topping
1 (16-ounce) package chocolate sandwich cookies, crushed
15 clear small plastic cups
30 chocolate chips

Combine the milk and pudding mix in a large bowl. Beat with a wire whisk for 2 minutes. Fold in 3 cups of the whipped topping and half the crushed cookies. Spoon into the cups and top with the remaining crushed cookies. Decorate each cup with a large spoonful of whipped topping to resemble a ghost. Place 2 chocolate chips on each whipped topping ghost to resemble eyes. Chill until serving time.

Yield: 15 boo cups

GREAT IDEA!

Make spider ice cubes by freezing small plastic spiders in ice cube trays. Serve the cubes in soft drinks or juice for a spooky surprise. This should not be served to young children.

BATTY CHICKEN

• Boneless, skinless chicken breast
• Eggs, beaten
• Seasoned bread crumbs

Pound the chicken with a meat mallet until very thin. Cut out bat shapes using a bat-shaped cookie cutter or a sharp knife. Dip the chicken into the eggs and coat with the bread crumbs. Place on a greased baking sheet. Bake at 350 degrees for 20 to 25 minutes.

Yield: variable

BROOMSTICK BROWNIES

4   ounces unsweetened baking chocolate
3/4 cup (1 1/2 sticks) butter or margarine
2   cups sugar
4   eggs
1   cup flour
2 1/2 cups cold milk
2   (4-ounce) packages vanilla instant pudding mix
•   Yellow and red food coloring

Combine the chocolate and butter in a large microwave-safe mixer bowl. Microwave on High for 2 minutes, stirring until the chocolate is completely melted. Stir the sugar into the chocolate mixture. Beat in the eggs and flour. Spread in a greased 9x13-inch baking pan. Bake at 350 degrees for 30 to 35 minutes. Remove from the oven and immediately punch holes 1 inch apart in the hot brownies with the round handle of a wooden spoon.

Combine the milk and pudding mix in a large bowl. Beat with a wire whisk for 1 minute. Stir in 2 drops of yellow food coloring and 4 drops of red food coloring. Mix well until the pudding mixture is orange. Pour half the pudding mixture into holes in the brownies. Let the remaining pudding stand to thicken. Swirl over the top of the brownies. Chill, covered, for 1 hour.

Yield: 24 brownies

WITCH HAT COOKIES

1   tube orange decorator frosting
1   package plain chocolate cookies
•   Chocolate candy kisses

Place a dot of frosting in the center of each cookie. Attach a chocolate candy kiss to the frosting. Let stand for 30 minutes or until the frosting has dried completely. Attach the decorator tip to the tube of orange frosting. Draw a bow around each candy kiss with the frosting.

Yield: variable

Cool Spider Treats

12 chocolate cupcakes
16 ounces whipped topping
• Chocolate candy sprinkles
• Black or chocolate licorice candy strands
24 round orange candies (Skittles work well here)

Frost the bottom of the cupcakes with the whipped topping. Sprinkle with chocolate sprinkles. Insert the licorice through the frosting and into the cupcakes at the edges, bending downward to resemble spider legs. Top each cupcake with 2 pieces of orange candy for the eyes.

Yield: 12 cool spider treats

GREAT IDEA!

Make a pumpkin town out of several pumpkins. Clean out the inside of the pumpkins and carve out windows and doors. Decorate the borders with glitter glue. Light the pumpkin houses with candles or with flashlights.

Make Goblin Snack Mix using chocolate-covered pretzels, miniature chocolate chip cookies, candy-coated peanut butter pieces, Halloween "M&M's" chocolate candies, and orange slice candies. Put the mix in small Halloween goodie bags and give as a treat on Halloween night.

For a fun, easy Halloween dessert, top Chocolate Cupcakes with prepared orange frosting. Decorate the top with gummy worms, candy corns, or candy pumpkins, or use a favorite Halloween candy.

Gobbler Goodies

1/4   cup (1/2 stick) butter or margarine
4   cups miniature marshmallows
6   cups crisp rice cereal
28   chocolate sandwich cookies
1 1/2 cups chocolate frosting
1   (12-ounce) package candy corn

Melt the butter in a saucepan. Add the marshmallows. Cook over low heat until melted, stirring constantly. Stir in the cereal. Remove from the heat and let cool for 10 minutes.

Form the cereal into twenty-eight 1 1/2-inch balls with buttered hands. Twist apart the sandwich cookies. Spread the frosting on each cookie half and use 28 of the halves as the base for each turkey.

Place each cereal ball on top of a frosted cookie half, pressing to adhere. Press 3 pieces of candy corn in a fan pattern on each remaining cookie half.

Press each cookie half into a cereal ball to form a tail. Attach candy corn with frosting to form the turkey's head.

Yield: 28 gobbler goodies

Note: Our Nutrition instructor turned the recipe contribution into a contest for our 24 students. They all prepared their favorite recipes, tasted them, and then voted. The winner was Mandi Weaver and her recipe for Gobbler Goodies. This recipe is being submitted by the English Nanny & Governess School in Chagrin Falls, Ohio.

—Sheilagh G. Roth
Executive Director

148

PUMPKIN SQUARES

1   (16-ounce) package pound
     cake mix
3   eggs
2   tablespoons (1/4 stick) butter,
     melted
4   teaspoons pumpkin pie spice
8   ounces cream cheese, softened
1   (14-ounce) can sweetened
     condensed milk
1   (16-ounce) can pumpkin
1/2 teaspoon salt
1   cup chopped pecans

Combine the cake mix, 1 of the eggs, melted butter and 2 teaspoons of the pumpkin pie spice in a large mixer bowl. Beat at low speed until the mixture is crumbly. Press over the bottom of a lightly buttered 10x15-inch baking pan. Set aside.

Beat the cream cheese in a large mixer bowl until light and fluffy. Beat in the condensed milk gradually. Add the remaining 2 eggs, 2 teaspoons pumpkin pie spice, pumpkin and salt. Beat until well blended.

Pour the mixture into the prepared pan and sprinkle with the pecans. Bake at 350 degrees for 30 to 35 minutes or until set. Chill, covered. Cut into small squares to serve. Store in the refrigerator.

Yield: 3 to 4 dozen squares

GREAT IDEA!

Cover the children's table with white butcher block paper and give them crayons. Suggest they make drawings of a meal while they wait on the real meal. This is an activity and a tablecloth in one!

Entertain children while cooking. Let them create a turkey while they wait on the meal. Give children a cored apple or pear half to use as a turkey's body, wooden picks, and small food such as raisins, chopped celery, cherries, and marshmallows for creating heads and tails.

150

SAGE CORN BREAD DRESSING

3   cups crumbled corn bread
2   cups dried bread crumbs
2   cups chicken broth
2   hard-cooked eggs, chopped
2   large onions, finely chopped
1   cup finely chopped celery
1/2 cup (1 stick) butter or margarine, melted
1   tablespoon whole dried sage, crushed

Combine the corn bread, bread crumbs, chicken broth, eggs, onions, celery, melted butter and sage in a large bowl and mix well. Spoon the mixture into a lightly greased 9x13-inch baking dish. Bake, uncovered, at 325 degrees for 1 hour or until golden brown.

Yield: 8 to 10 servings

SWEET POTATO BISCUITS

1   cup flour
2   tablespoons baking powder
2   tablespoons sugar
$1/2$ teaspoon salt
$1/3$ cup shortening
1   cup mashed cooked sweet
     potatoes
2   tablespoons milk

Combine the flour, baking powder, sugar and salt in a large bowl. Cut in the shortening until the mixture is crumbly. Add the sweet potatoes and mix well. Sprinkle the milk over the mixture and stir until just moistened. Roll the dough on a heavily floured surface to $1/2$-inch thickness. Cut with a 2-inch biscuit cutter. Place on a lightly greased baking sheet. Bake at 450 degrees for 10 minutes or until light brown.

Yield: 1 dozen biscuits

GREAT IDEA!

Keep in touch with relatives over the holidays. Cut turkey feathers out of construction paper and mail them to your relatives with a note asking them to write what they are thankful for that year on the feathers and mail them back to you. Create a turkey body and tape the feathers on the turkey as they are returned to you. See how full you can get your turkey.

151

Decorate plain glass ornaments using paint pens of different colors.

Make a candy tree by gluing wrapped hard candies to plastic-foam balls. Stick the balls on dowels. Insert the dowels in florist's foam in a decorated pot and tie with ribbons. Use different colored candies and ribbons.

152

CANDY POPCORN DESSERT

10   cups popped popcorn
1½   cups red and green gumdrops
2   cups peanuts
½   cup (1 stick) plus 1 tablespoon butter
½   cup canola oil
1   (16-ounce) package marshmallows

Combine the popcorn, gumdrops and peanuts in a large bowl. Melt the butter in a medium saucepan. Add the canola oil and marshmallows. Cook until the marshmallows are melted, stirring constantly. Pour the marshmallow mixture over the popcorn mixture. Stir gently until the popcorn is well coated. Spoon the mixture into a buttered 10-inch springform pan. Let stand for 2 hours. Loosen the side of the pan with a spatula and remove carefully.

Yield: 16 servings

Note: Wrap the cooled dessert in tinted plastic wrap and tie with ribbon for a festive holiday gift. May also wrap individual slices.

Gingerbread Sweets

1 1/3 cups flour
1 1/2 teaspoons ground ginger
1 teaspoon cinnamon
1/8 teaspoon salt
5 tablespoons unsalted butter, softened
1/3 cup sugar
1/2 cup molasses
1 teaspoon baking soda
1/2 cup boiling water
2 eggs
• Confectioners' sugar

Combine the flour, ginger, cinnamon and salt in a medium bowl. Combine the butter and sugar in a large mixer bowl and beat until light and fluffy. Add the molasses to the butter mixture and stir until well blended. Stir the baking soda into the boiling water and beat into the butter mixture. Add the flour mixture to the butter mixture gradually and stir until well blended. Beat the eggs into the batter.

Spray 12 cupcake-sized star-shaped muffin cups with nonstick cooking spray. Spoon the batter into the muffin cups. Bake at 350 degrees for 35 minutes. Remove to a wire rack to cool. Sprinkle with confectioners' sugar.

Yield: 12 gingerbread sweets

153

154

PRETZEL GARLAND

- Pretzel knots dipped in white chocolate
- 1 (3-foot) holiday ribbon

Thread 1 pretzel onto the ribbon and securely tie the ribbon to the pretzel in a knot. Repeat, spacing the pretzels evenly at desired intervals and securely tying each pretzel with a knot. Hang the garland on a tree, mantel, wall, or door for a fun, easy holiday decoration. Use pretzels dipped in dark chocolate or green- and red-tinted chocolate for a festive variety.

PULL-APART CHRISTMAS BREAD

1/2 cup sugar
2 to 3 teaspoons cinnamon
1 (1-pound) package frozen bread dough, thawed
1/2 cup (1 stick) butter, melted

Combine the sugar and cinnamon in a small bowl and mix well. Shape the dough into 1-inch balls. Dip the dough balls in the melted butter and roll in the sugar-cinnamon mixture to coat. Place the dough balls in a 9-inch round pan sprayed with nonstick cooking spray so they are just touching. Place a small damp towel over the pan and let rise for 1 hour or until doubled in bulk. Bake at 375 degrees for 30 minutes or until golden brown. Invert to a serving plate and serve warm, pulling the bread apart with hands.

Yield: 6 to 8 servings

ROLL-OUT CHRISTMAS COOKIES

1   cup (2 sticks) butter, softened
3/4 cup sugar
3/4 cup vegetable oil
2   eggs
1   cup confectioners' sugar
2   teaspoons vanilla extract
1   teaspoon baking soda
1   teaspoon cream of tartar
1/2 teaspoon salt
4 1/2 cups flour
•   Tinted sugar
•   Christmas decorator candies

Cream the butter and sugar in a mixer bowl. Add the oil and eggs and beat well. Beat in the confectioners' sugar, vanilla, baking soda, cream of tartar and salt. Add the flour, stirring until well blended. Chill, covered, for at least 2 hours. Roll out on a heavily floured surface to the desired thickness. Cut out with holiday-theme cutters. Sprinkle with tinted sugar and decorator candies. Place on a lightly greased cookie sheet. Bake at 350 degrees for 10 minutes or until golden brown.

Yield: 4 dozen cookies

Note: Try using different shaped cookie cutters for holiday fun. Use Christmas trees, bells, candy canes, angels and snowflakes. Decorate the cookies according to their shape. Use decorator frosting and make stripes on the candy canes and wings and a halo for the angels. These make beautiful and enjoyable gifts for neighbors, teachers and friends. The size of the cookie cutters used will affect the yield.

GREAT IDEA!

Make Cinnamon Christmas Cider by combining 4 cups apple cider and 1/4 cup red hot cinnamon candies in a saucepan. Bring to a boil and simmer until the candies are melted, stirring occasionally. Serve hot or cold.

Make candy cane spoons by painting long-handled wooden spoons with red and green stripes. Tie on a pretty ribbon and these make great home-made gifts!

Make jolly pots by decorating tiny terra-cotta pots. Let children paint designs on the pots using acrylic paint or paint pens. Attach a pretty holiday ribbon and spray paint silver or gold for an added sheen. Fill the pots with tiny surprises such as toy dinosaurs, cookie cutters, or holiday candy. Display them on a mantel or in a window, or give as gifts.

COZY COCOA MIXTURE

8   cups instant dry milk
1   (16-ounce) package instant cocoa
     mix
1   cup confectioners' sugar
1   cup nondairy dry coffee creamer

Combine the instant dry milk, cocoa mix, confectioners' sugar and dry coffee creamer in a 1-gallon plastic airtight container; mix well. Combine 1/4 cup of the mixture and 1 cup of hot water for each serving. Store in an airtight container.

Yield: 32 servings

156

Make a Festive Picture Frame

- Photo
- Acrylic, plastic or wooden frame
- Gold paint pen or permanent marker

Place a favorite picture of the children in a white, red or green acrylic, plastic or wooden picture frame. Any size frame will work. Pictures of children with Santa Claus or dressed in holiday outfits are especially cute. Write a short holiday message on the top or bottom edge of the frame using a gold paint pen or other permanent marker that writes well on various surfaces. Some festive suggestions are "Oh, what fun," "Happy Holidays," "Happy Hanukkah" or "Joy to the World." This makes a wonderful gift for parents, grandparents or other friends and family.

Give a Napkin the Holiday Spirit

- Red or green cloth napkin
- Artificial holly
- Doily
- Ribbon
- Candy cane
- Small jingle bells

Roll a napkin in the desired style. Red or green cloth napkins look especially festive, or you can use a large paper napkin. Tie the rolled napkin with a sprig of artificial holly. Wrap a small doily around the napkin and tie with some holiday ribbon. Tuck a candy cane into the rolled napkin and hook on some small jingle bells. Repeat the process until you have enough rolled napkins for each place setting. This is fun for the kids to help do and gives dinnertime an added festive touch.

157

MOVE OVER, PICASSO

CRAFTS

For a fun outdoor craft, have the children

lie down on the driveway or sidewalk and, using

colored chalk, draw the outline of their bodies.

Let the children do each other

and the grown-ups as well—it will be fun for all!

When finished, let them color in their faces, hair, clothing,

accessories, etc., to match what they have on,

or they can make up stuff. Make sure to take a photo

of both the real people and colorful images

that the children create.

KELLIE GERES—INA 1997 NANNY OF THE YEAR

BEAD NECKLACE

1/2 cup plus 2 tablespoons warm
   water
1/2 cup salt
• Bowl
1 1/2 cups flour
• Round wooden pick
• Aluminum foil
• Baking sheet
• Colored markers or watercolors
• Small watercolor brush
• Waxed dental floss
• Pencil

Pour the water over the salt in a large bowl, stirring to dissolve completely. Add the flour and mix until smooth. Let stand until cool enough to handle. Knead the mixture until very firm and smooth. Shape into beads no larger than a marble. Pierce a hole through the center of each bead with a round wooden pick, wiggling the pick to enlarge the hole slightly. Arrange the beads on a foil-lined baking sheet.

Bake the beads at 250 degrees for 1 1/4 hours or until completely firm. Let stand until cool. Color with markers or paint with watercolors using a small brush. Let stand until dry.

Cut an 18-inch length of dental floss; fold over 1 inch at the end and press to stiffen it. Tie a pencil to the other end to keep the beads from sliding off. Pass the floss through the holes in the beads. Remove the pencil from the end and tie the ends together to form a necklace.

BAKER'S CLAY MEDALLIONS

4   cups flour
1 1/2 cups water
1   cup salt
• Bowl
• Cookie cutters
• Plastic straw, pencil or skewer
• Baking sheet
• Tempera paints
• Brush
• Clear spray varnish
• Ribbons or cords

Combine the flour, water and salt in a bowl and mix well. Knead for 5 to 10 minutes or until smooth. Roll 1/4 inch thick on a work surface. Cut as desired with cookie cutters. Pierce a hole near 1 edge with a plastic straw, pencil or skewer. Arrange on a baking sheet.

Bake at 250 degrees for 2 hours or until firm. Let stand until cool. Paint with tempera paints. Let stand until dry. Spray with varnish. String on ribbons or cords for necklaces or holiday decorations.

161

*Need a smock for a messy project? Cut two holes for arms
and one for the head in an old pillowcase and slip it on the little artist.
Don't forget that Dad's old shirts work well too!*

Bubble Level Tube

- Glue
- 2 corks, 1 inch in diameter
- 1 clear plastic tube, 1 inch in diameter
- 2 tablespoons vegetable oil
- Food coloring
- Water
- Small craft items such as fish, shells and/or animals
- Glitter and/or sand

Glue 1 cork in 1 end of the tube. Let stand until dry. Hold the tube with the cork end down and add the oil, food coloring and enough water to nearly fill the tube.

Add the fish or other craft items and glitter or sand. Fill the tube the rest of the way with water. Glue the remaining cork in the end and let stand until dry.

Bubble Print Cards

- Scissors
- Stock paper
- Bubble solution
- Bowls
- Tempera paints
- Straw

Cut the stock paper into rectangles and fold over to form note cards. Place 1 cup bubble solution in a separate plastic bowl for each color desired. Add 2 tablespoons tempera paint to each bowl and mix well.

Use a straw to blow bubbles in each bowl. Place the note card carefully on the bubbles to create circular designs. Let stand until dry.

Soap Bubbles

2   cups warm water
1   tablespoon sugar
2   tablespoons liquid detergent
1   tablespoon glycerin
•   Shallow bowl
•   Wire loops, fly swatters or plastic collars from soda 6-packs

Combine the water, sugar; detergent and glycerin in a shallow bowl and mix well. Dip wire loops, fly swatters or plastic collars into the mixture and blow to make bubbles.

Note: Dawn or Joy detergent work best in this mixture, and the glycerin makes the bubbles iridescent. As a kid, you would have given a week's allowance for this recipe. Pass it on!

Make a chalk adventure trail. Start at the driveway and make the trail lead to the front or back door. This will be fun for Mom or Dad to find their way through as they get home from work. The trail can be long and winding or through a scary or enchanting forest. Be sure someone meets Mom or Dad at the door to help them through the maze.

Color Your World— And Fingers Too

Color Your Pasta for Jewelry

- 3   to 4 tablespoons rubbing alcohol
- Food coloring paste
- Bowl
- Uncooked macaroni, or other tube-shaped pasta
- Waxed paper
- Cords

Combine the alcohol with a small amount of desired food coloring in a bowl and mix until smooth. Add the pasta and mix gently to color. Spread on waxed paper and let stand until dry. String on cords to create necklaces and bracelets.

Color Your Sand

- Clean fine sand
- Jars
- Powdered tempera paints

Place sand in a jar and add enough tempera paint to create the desired color, mixing well. Repeat the process in separate jars for additional colors. Store in the jars to use in your sand painting projects.

Color Your String

- String or rope
- Tempera paint
- Paper or waxed paper

Dip the string or rope into tempera paint. Arrange in desired designs on paper for string art, or place on waxed paper and let stand until dry for colorful wrap for packages.

CREATIVE DOUGH

1   cup water
•   Several drops of food coloring
•   Saucepan
1   cup flour
2   teaspoons cream of tartar
1   tablespoon vegetable oil
$1/3$ teaspoon salt
1   teaspoon vanilla extract or other appealing scent
•   Airtight container

Combine the water and food coloring in a saucepan. Add the flour, cream of tartar, oil, salt and vanilla and mix well. Cook over medium heat for 5 minutes or until the mixture forms a ball, stirring constantly.

Remove to a work surface and let stand for 5 minutes or until cool enough to handle. Knead for 30 seconds or until smooth. Cool completely. Store in an airtight container in the refrigerator.

Note: This dough has the added sensory attraction of aroma, but remember, it's still not edible.

165

PEANUT BUTTER PLAY DOUGH

- Nonstick cooking spray
- Bowl
- $^1/_4$ cup honey
- $^1/_4$ cup nonfat dry milk powder
- 6 tablespoons peanut butter
- $^1/_2$ cup crushed crisp rice cereal

Spray a bowl with nonstick cooking spray. Add the honey and dry milk powder to the bowl and mix well. Add the peanut butter and mix until smooth. Stir in the cereal. Use as edible modeling clay.

Note: To serve as a snack, shape the peanut butter mixture into $^1/_2$-inch balls and roll in the cereal. Dip into melted chocolate if desired. Store in the refrigerator.

PLAY CLAY

- 1 pound baking soda
- 1 cup cornstarch
- 1$^1/_4$ cups water
- Saucepan

Combine the baking soda, cornstarch and water in a saucepan and mix well. Cook over medium heat until thickened and smooth, stirring constantly. Cool completely. Store in an airtight container in the refrigerator.

Note: To increase the recipe, use 3 pounds baking soda, 1 pound cornstarch and 4 cups water.

Play restaurant at the dinner table. Let the children be the customers and the grown-up be the waitress. Inform the customers of the "special" of the day and take their order on a real notebook. The customers could leave a tip on the table if the service was especially good. It could be pretend money or a special toy.

EDIBLE FINGER PAINT

- Tape
- Finger painting or butcher's paper
1 large can of spray whipped topping
- Food coloring

Tape the paper to an outside table, preferably near a hose. Shake up the can of whipped topping and spray it on the paper.

Add the food coloring to the whipped topping and spread with fingers to make a painting—and snack.

HOMEMADE FINGER PAINT

$1/2$ cup cornstarch
3 tablespoons sugar
2 cups cold water
- Heavy saucepan
- Bowls
- Food coloring
- Liquid detergent

Combine the cornstarch, sugar and water in a heavy saucepan and mix well. Cook over low heat until thickened and smooth, stirring constantly.

Divide the mixture into 4 or 5 equal portions and place in bowls. Add food coloring and 1 scant teaspoon of detergent to each portion and mix well. Let cool completely before letting the children start creating those treasured masterpieces.

167

Gooey Goop

1¹/₂ teaspoons borax powder
1 cup water
• Large bowl
8 ounces white craft glue
1 cup water
• Tempera paint
• Medium bowl
• Airtight plastic container

Combine the borax powder and 1 cup water in a large bowl and stir to dissolve the borax. Combine the glue, 1 cup water and several drops of paint in a medium bowl and mix until smooth. Add to the borax mixture and mix well; mixture will form a glob that can be kneaded and squeezed. Store in an airtight plastic container.

Note: Borax powder can be found in the laundry detergent section of most supermarkets. Do not eat the goop or allow it to come in contact with eyes, clothing, carpets or upholstery. Rinse immediately with warm water to remove from fabric. Do not pour leftover goop down the drain.

FROSTED GLASS VOTIVES

- Small glass jars
- Colored nail polish
- Clear nail polish
- Table salt
- Votive candles

Wash and dry the jars well, removing labels and glue. Decorate the jars using nail polish to create designs or cover the entire surface by blending or layering the polish. Let stand until the polish is dry.

Cover the surface of the jars with a coat of clear nail polish and let stand until the polish is tacky. Sprinkle with salt to frost and let stand until completely dry. Brush gently to remove the loose salt. Place a candle in each jar.

Make a special "book on video" for faraway relatives. Grandparents especially love this homemade gift. Select favorite bedtime stories. Set up a video camera and make sure the child is wearing his or her favorite pajamas. Give an introduction to the story and then let the child read the story while you are videotaping. Be sure to wish the recipient a "good-night" or "happy birthday." You could also include the copy of the book that was read with the video that you are sending.

LAVA BOTTLES

- Clear (12- to 16-ounce) plastic bottles with tops
- Light corn syrup
- Food coloring
- Glitter, sequins and other craft items
- Water
- Glue and glue gun

Wash the bottles, removing the labels and glue. Pour 1/4 cup corn syrup and the desired amount of food coloring into each bottle. Add the glitter and/or other craft items and fill the bottles with water.

Glue the top on securely with the hot glue gun. Let stand until dry. Shake the mixture and invert to watch the items move through the bottle.

170

*Packing a child's lunch for school? Carve a short note or name
into the side of a banana with a dull object, not tearing the banana skin.
It will turn brown and show up very well by lunchtime.*

MASKS

- Scissors
- 1 heavy paper plate
- Tape
- Paper cups
- Buttons
- Newspaper
- Warm water
- 1 cup flour
- Bowl
- Brush
- Tempera paint
- Glue
- Yarn
- Bottle caps

Cut holes in the paper plate for the eyes and mouth. Tape pieces of the paper cups and buttons to the plate to provide shape for the cheeks and nose. Cut the newspaper into 2-inch strips.

Add water gradually to the flour in a bowl, mixing to form a paste the consistency of white craft glue. Brush several strips of newspaper at a time with the paste. Press over the surface of the plate, covering the entire plate with several layers of newspaper.

Let dry for 8 hours or longer. Paint the mask as desired. Glue the yarn into place for the hair and the bottle caps for earrings.

MOCK CHALK

8 cups plaster of Paris
4 cups warm water
• Bowl
• Powdered tempera paint
• Waxed paper
• Cardboard toilet paper tubes
• Tape

Combine the plaster of Paris and water in a large bowl. Add the desired amount of tempera paint and mix well. Line the toilet paper tube with waxed paper and seal 1 end securely with tape. Pour in the plaster of Paris mixture and tap the tube to release any air bubbles. Let stand until hard. Repeat the process for each stick of chalk.

Note: This chalk is perfect for sidewalk art. It can also be used to create great powdered paint. Crush the chalk into powder with a spoon and apply it with a wet paintbrush.

POSTCARD FLIP BOOK

• Postcards
• Pencil or pen
• Hole punch
2 large silver rings

Purchase a postcard for each day or stop of a family trip. Ask the child to write a favorite memory of the day or place pictured; smaller children may need to dictate to an adult.

Punch 2 holes in the top of each postcard and slip it onto the rings. This is both a good entertainment and a treasured memory.

CREEPY GLOVE PUPPET

- 1   inexpensive (1-size-fits-all) stretch glove
- •   Self-adhesive Velcro fasteners, cut into small circles or squares
- •   Small plastic or rubber Halloween creepy critters, such as spiders, bats, scorpions and bugs

Place the glove on the child's hand. Place 1 side of the Velcro fasteners on each finger. Apply the matching sides of the fasteners to the underside of the creepy critters. Stick the critters to the glove.

EASY PUPPET STAGE

- 1   tension rod or chinning bar
- 1   sheet or piece of fabric large enough to double over the rod

Place the tension rod or chinning bar about halfway down in a doorway that allows space in front of it for the audience. Drape the sheet or fabric over the rod. Players position themselves behind the sheet to operate the puppets above the rod.

Write a variety of words on flash cards, including verbs, nouns, articles, and adjectives. Just write one word per card. Shuffle the words and let children create sentences and phrases with the cards such as "The red ball rolled down the hill." This activity is primarily for younger children learning to read and write.

Scratch Board

- Crayons
1 (8x10-inch or 5x7-inch) poster board
- Black poster paint
- Brush
- Nail file or other object for scratching

Color the poster board with the crayons, using various colors and covering completely. Paint the poster board with the black paint, covering completely. Let stand until dry. Use the nail file to scratch a design through the black paint to reveal the colored layer.

Note: Mistakes can be painted over and redone.

Secret Messages

- Waxed paper
- White paper
- Pen
- Colored pencils

Place a sheet of waxed paper waxed side down on a sheet of white paper. Write a message on the waxed paper with the pen, pressing down hard enough to transfer the wax to the white paper.

To read the secret message, rub a colored pencil across the paper; the wax will resist the color and the message will be revealed.

SHAKER BOTTLES

4   (16-ounce) plastic soda bottles
4   packages colored beads

Wash the bottles and dry completely. Place the contents of a bead package into each bottle and seal tightly. Shake to make music.

SPLATTER PAINT GIFT WRAP

1   plastic liner, drop cloth or old shower curtain
1   wastebasket
•   Masking tape
•   Finger painting paper
•   Paint
•   Brushes

Spread the plastic liner outside or on an out-of-the-way floor area and place the wastebasket in the center. Tape 1 piece of paper at a time to the inside rim of the wastebasket. Drip and splatter the paint onto the paper in the desired patterns. Hang the papers to dry.

Note: This is a good activity to do outside and clean up in the sprinkler or pool.

SHOOTING STAR WANDS

- Pen
- Aluminum foil pie plate
- Scissors
1 (12-inch) length of heavy wire
- Permanent markers
- Nail polish
- Glitter

Draw a star shape with a 1½-inch tail on the bottom of the pie plate. Cut out the star and tail. Bend a small loop in the end of the wire and wrap the tail of the star around the loop; crimp securely. Decorate with markers or paint with nail polish and sprinkle with glitter.

Note: A bouquet of shooting stars would add a fun decorative touch to a planter, or even your dining room table.

176

Help children write their own cookbook. Let them pick the recipes that go in the book and even write them in their own words. It could be as simple as, "Take a hot dog out of the fridge, put in boiling water, place on bun and eat!" Or recipes could include favorites that grown-ups make for the children. This is a fun and easy way to make dinner special for everyone, especially when the children get to pick the dinner menu out of their own book.

A String of Stars Photo Frames

- Scissors
- Ribbon
- Stapler and staples
- Heavy construction paper
- Glue
- Glitter
- Small photos
- Cord

Cut a piece of ribbon long enough to hold the number of frames to be made. Fold over 1 end of the ribbon about 1 inch and staple to make a hanging loop.

Cut 2 identical stars from the construction paper for each frame. Staple half the stars to the ribbon to serve as photo backs, spacing evenly.

Cut a circle from the centers of the remaining stars to serve as photo frames. Decorate the frames with glitter. Position the photos behind the opening and glue to the photo backs. Let stand until dry. Thread a piece of cord through the ribbon loop and hang.

Note: Your own "String of Stars" will look great hung from a doorknob, bedpost or tree branch.

177

SUNFLYER

- Scissors
1 large yellow plastic dinner plate
- Glue
1 white paper dessert plate
- Buttons in various colors, sizes and shapes
1 narrow (12-inch-long) ribbon
3 wide green (24-inch-long) ribbons

Snip triangles from the rim of the yellow plate to create a flower petal design. Invert the white plate and glue to the center of the yellow plate for the center of the flower. Let stand until dry.

Glue the buttons over the surface of the white plate. Let stand until dry. Glue the narrow ribbon to 1 edge of the back of the plate to use as a hanger. Glue the wide green ribbons to the bottom of the plate. Hang the plate where the ribbons can fly in the wind.

Recommended Practices

for Nanny Placement Agencies

Recommended Practices

for Nannies

Recommended Competencies

for the Education of Nannies

Recommended Practices
for Nanny Placement Agencies

To promote quality child care and
an environment for all children that nurtures their well-being,
the International Nanny Association recommends the
following practices for nanny placement agencies.

RELATIONSHIPS WITH FAMILIES

Disclose the method of interviewing candidates referred for in-home child care positions. INA recommends that candidates be interviewed in person. When personal interviews are not possible, the prospective employer should be advised that the candidate was interviewed and which interview method was used; i.e., by telephone, an agent acting on behalf of the agency.

Check candidate's personal and employment references. INA recommends that the family be provided with information on a candidate's employment history. At a minimum, two references should be checked by telephone. The agency should disclose all information about the candidate verified through personal and employment references, as allowed by law. Families may be offered the opportunity to check references for themselves.

Provide information on the candidate's job qualifications to the prospective employer. At a minimum, INA recommends that the agency accurately disclose to the prospective employer information obtained on a candidate's references, social security verification, criminal check, driver's license check, and the methodology used to obtain the information, as allowed by law.

Prepare a written agreement with each client family, which specifies the agency's fees, refund/replacement policies, and services to be provided by the agency. INA recommends that a written agreement or contract be drafted between the agency and the family to facilitate an understanding of the obligations of both parties. Both the agency and the family should keep a copy.

Make adjustments/refunds promptly and in accordance with the written policies of the agency. INA recommends that time periods within which replacement and/or refunds will be made by the agency be clearly outlined in the written agreement between the family and the agency. Any other conditions regarding replacements or refunds, such as limits on the number of replacements or amounts that will be refunded, should also be included.

RELATIONSHIPS WITH NANNIES

Respect and regard nannies as clients. INA recommends that agencies regard nannies with the same respect as client families by considering each nanny's preferences and qualifications when making referrals to prospective employers.

Accurately and truthfully describe job duties and responsibilities, working conditions, hours, salary, and benefits for in-home child care opportunities. INA recommends that all information used to promote the in-home child care profession depict job possibilities, including salaries and benefits, accurately. When a nanny asks an agency about positions available, INA recommends that only currently available jobs be described. The description of job duties, hours, salary, and benefits of a proposed position should be based on information available to the agency for a current, bona fide opening.

Help the nanny develop a written work agreement that accurately describes the conditions of employment arranged with the family. INA recommends that agencies ensure that all terms of employment in the home agreed to by families and nannies be summarized in the form of a written work agreement. At a minimum, INA recommends that a work agreement include: job duties; hours and days of duty; salary amount; when and how paid, and compensation for overtime worked; employer's legally required tax obligations; fringe benefits such as health insurance, holiday and vacation policies, sick leave if offered; probationary period; frequency of work agreement review; terms of notice of termination and grounds for dismissal.

Provide a written explanation to nanny candidates regarding applicable fees and/or agency services to job applicants prior to rendering services. INA recommends the agency inform any candidates in writing of the agency's obligations to the nanny prior to and after placement. Such an explanation of services should include fees, if any, to be paid by the applicant, the agency's responsibility to the nanny in the event a placement is unsuccessful,

and the agency's policies regarding payment for travel costs for interviews or relocation to accept a job.

Make family information available to nanny candidates. INA recommends that agencies provide nanny candidates with descriptive information on prospective employer families. In addition to details pertaining to the available position, such information might include child-rearing philosophy, a family profile, special interests and needs, and family references.

GENERAL PRACTICES

Respect the work agreements in force between families and nannies. INA recommends that nanny applicants not be solicited for other positions while they are still in the employ of a family, unless the nanny requests assistance with finding a new position.

Respect the proprietary, promotional, or company-sensitive materials of other agencies. INA recommends that agencies independently develop all materials related to the operation of their business. If others' forms, brochures, training manuals, or other printed materials are used, permission should always be obtained in writing and the source of materials acknowledged.

Abide by all pertinent laws and regulations. INA recommends that agencies be knowledgeable about and comply with all applicable laws and regulations affecting placement operations in their jurisdictions, including but not limited to licensing requirements, immigration laws, and wage and labor requirements. INA requires placement agencies to carry professional insurance if obtainable.

Recommended Practices for Nannies

To promote quality child care and
an environment for all children that nurtures their well-being,
the International Nanny Association recommends the
following practices for nannies.

PROFESSIONALISM

Participate in personal and professional growth activities. INA recommends that nannies become involved in social, cultural, and educational activities not only to maintain and improve their child care skills, but also to enhance their own personal growth. Suggested activities include professional development classes, seminars and training programs, participation in career-related professional organizations, and involvement in community affairs.

Act as an advocate for young children. INA recommends that nannies promote knowledge and understanding of young children, and their needs and rights. Nannies should be familiar with the signs of child abuse and neglect, and be knowledgeable of procedures for dealing with them.

RELATIONSHIPS WITH CHILDREN

Respect each child as a unique individual. INA recommends that nannies recognize the individuality of the child/children in their care by creating an environment that fosters trust, self-esteem, and independence in children, and by using consistent daily routines and developmentally appropriate behavior management techniques.

Provide developmentally appropriate play and learning experiences. INA recommends that nannies provide for the physical, emotional, intellectual, and social needs of children by using developmentally appropriate play/learning activities, materials, and equipment.

Create and maintain a safe and healthy environment for children. INA recommends that nannies promote the physical and emotional well-being of children. Duties may include: serving nutritious meals and snacks; supervising rest periods, naps, and sleep; recognizing symptoms of common childhood illnesses; handling emergency situations; administering first aid; teaching children the hygienic way to bathe and wash hands, hair, and teeth; taking every safety precaution when traveling with children; performing domestic tasks related to the care and maintenance of the child's areas of the home such as bedroom, playroom, bathroom, and outside play space; laundering and making simple repairs to children's clothing; and observing safety rules in the home.

Communicate effectively at the child's level of understanding. INA recommends that nannies model appropriate language for children, recognize stages of language development in children, and engage in activities that encourage language development.

RELATIONSHIPS WITH PARENTS/EMPLOYERS

Request a personal interview with prospective employers. INA recommends that nannies interview prospective employers in person, preferably in the family's home.

Request a descriptive, written work agreement detailing conditions of employment. INA recommends that, at a minimum, a work agreement include the following: job duties, hours and days of duty, salary amount, when and how paid and compensation for overtime worked, employer's legally required tax obligations, fringe benefits such as health insurance, holiday, and vacation policies, sick leave if offered, probationary period, frequency of work agreement review, terms of notice and termination and grounds for dismissal.

Respect the family's right to privacy. INA recommends that nannies show good judgment in maintaining confidentiality about the private lives of the families for whom they work.

Support the childrearing philosophy of the employer. INA recommends that nannies recognize the ultimate authority of parents in making decisions about the welfare and care of their child/children by respecting the parent/employer's philosophy of child rearing.

Develop positive relationships with the family. INA recommends that nannies work cooperatively with the family, perform duties as agreed, communicate openly and effectively, show sensitivity to family situations, seek constructive solutions to problems, and maintain a consistent, positive attitude.

RELATIONSHIPS WITH AGENCIES

Be clear about placement agency services and required fees prior to using agency services. INA recommends that nannies obtain a full and complete explanation of agency services, expectations, requirements, and fees before becoming obligated to an agency.

Accurately and truthfully represent personal job qualifications and experience. INA recommends that nannies provide complete, accurate, and truthful information about their background, education, special skills and abilities, and prior work experience.

Request descriptive information about prospective employers. INA recommends that in addition to details about a particular position such as working hours, working conditions, salary, and benefits, nannies also obtain all information available about the employing family. A placement agency can provide details about family needs and preferences. They may also be able to supply the names and phone numbers of family references whom the nanny can contact if desired.

183

Recommended Competencies for the Education of Nannies

To promote quality child care and an environment for all children that nurtures their well-being, the International Nanny Association recommends that a nanny demonstrate the ability to perform competently in the following areas.

Competencies Related to Meeting the Developmental Needs of Children.

Observe and assess the behavior of children. Plan and implement consistent daily routines. Create an environment to foster trust, self-esteem, and independence in children. Utilize age-appropriate behavior management techniques in interaction with children. Plan and implement developmentally appropriate play/learning activities for children. Choose and care for developmentally appropriate play materials and equipment.

Competencies Related to Interaction with Parents/Employers, Family Dynamics.

Communicate effectively, both orally and in writing. Articulate a personal philosophy of child care. Maintain the confidentiality of the employing family. Demonstrate knowledge and understanding of parent/employer's philosophy of child rearing and recognize the special role a nanny assumes in becoming a part of the child rearing "team." Recognize the ultimate authority of parents in making decisions regarding the welfare and care of the child. Follow instructions and directions in a timely manner.

Competencies Related to Professionalism, Personal Development, and Social Skills.

Present a professional attitude and appearance. Use good judgment. Utilize appropriate language and manners. Demonstrate initiative in planning and performance of tasks and an ability to work unsupervised. Participate in career-related professional organizations. Participate in social, cultural, and educational activities to enhance personal growth and maintain and improve competency.

Competencies Related to Physical Care of Children.

Perform tasks related to the physical care of children. Maintain appropriate hygienic standards for children regarding bathing, hand washing, care of the hair and teeth. Feed, change, and bathe infants. Prepare infant feedings and care for feeding equipment. Select clothing appropriate to the child's physical/social activities. Plan and supervise rest, bed, and nap times. Plan and prepare nutritionally balanced meals and snacks. Care for the mildly ill child. Recognize symptoms of common childhood illnesses. Keep accurate records. Perform appropriate first aid techniques. Handle emergency situations. Observe appropriate safety precautions when traveling with children.

Competencies Related to Domestic Tasks and Care of the Child's Environment.

Perform domestic tasks related to care and maintenance of the child's areas of the home such as bedroom, playroom, bathroom, and outside play space. Launder and make simple repairs to children's clothing. Observe safety precautions appropriate to a private home.

ACKNOWLEDGMENTS

Board of Directors for 1998-1999

Mary O'Connor, President
Becky Kavanagh, 1st Vice President
Karen Stuke, 2nd Vice President
Colleen Grube, Secretary
Sandra Costantino, Treasurer

Annie Davis; Glenda Durst; Marsha Epstein
Alan Friedman; Kellie Geres; Sharon Graff-Radell
Barbara G. Kline; Pat Koester; Bluma K. Marder
Holly McManus; Wendy Sachs

185

Contributors

Jenny Adams	Sandra Goff	Jennifer Nield	Janet Schilling
Heidi Anderson	Harriette Grant	Mary O'Connor	Maryann Simila
Linda S. Balzer	Pat Guizdala	Diane O'Mara	Gail Smith
Ellen Beidler	Liza Holzbach	Nancy L. Osborne	Kathy Smith
Sandy Bell	Heidi H. Hupal	Kimberly Pargin	Jill Sneed
Louise Brown	Becky Kavanagh	Marissa Peitzman	Karen Snyder
Elaine Chastain	Heidi Killian	Janet Peter	Susan Stimmel
Mary Clurman	Pat Koester	Glenda Propst	Glenda Stouder
Tiffanie Compton	Heidi Kuehner	Ross Rainwater	Karen Stuke
Sandra Costantino	Jo Lambert	Suzanne	Betsy Von Dohlen
Dawn Crown	Angela Lehman	Rainwater	Mandi Weaver
Annie Davis	Kathleen Lott	Myra Rieck	Mary Weldon
Betty Davis	Pat Lynch	Joan Ross	Connie White
Susan Dineen	Bluma K. Marder	Sheilagh Roth	Shanna M. White
Gael Ann Dow	Mercedes Martinez	Rudi Rudolph	Cynthia Wilkinson
Kathy Dupuy	Katherine Matineo	Wendy Sachs	Beverly Wilson
Glenda Durst	Patsy Mason	Natalie Rose	Cindi Wingate
Joan Friedman	Michelle McNabb	Sanders	Rose Marie
Debbie Gardiner	Sloane H. Molby	Donna Saunders	Wooten
Kellie Geres	Sharon Mundell	Beth Schebler	Jenna Worsham

RECIPE INDEX

186

187

189

Non-Recipe Index

BEYOND PEANUT BUTTER AND JELLY

International Nanny Association
Member Services Office
900 Haddon Avenue, Suite 438
Collingswood, New Jersey 08108
www.nanny.org

Please send me _____ copies of Beyond Peanut Butter and Jelly @ $19.95 each $ _____

Postage and handling @ $4.95 each $ _____

Total $ _____

Name _____

Address _____

City _____ State _____ Zip _____

Method of Payment: [   ] Discover   [   ] MasterCard   [   ] VISA

[   ] Check payable to the International Nanny Association

Account Number _____ Expiration Date _____

Signature _____

Photocopies will be accepted.